Skin Deep

tattoos,

the disappearing West, very bad men,

and my deep love for them all

KAROL GRIFFIN

Harcourt, Inc.

orlando   austin   new york   san diego   toronto   london

Requests for permission to make copies of any part of the work
should be mailed to the following address: Permissions Department,
Harcourt, Inc., 6277 Sea Harbor Drive, Orlando, Florida 32887-6777.

www.HarcourtBooks.com

Chapter one of *Skin Deep* was previously published
in a slightly different form in *Northern Lights* and
Dorothy Parker's Elbow: Tattoos on Writers, Writers on Tattoos.
Chapter four also appeared in *Dorothy Parker's Elbow*
as "Grapefruit Flesh."

Library of Congress Cataloging-in-Publication Data
Griffin, Karol.
Skin deep: tattoos, the disappearing West, very bad men,
and my deep love for them all/Karol Griffin.—1st ed.
p.   cm.
ISBN 0-15-100884-1
1. Griffin, Karol. 2. Tattoo artists—Wyoming—Biography.
3. Tattooing—Wyoming—Wyoming. 4. Laramie (Wyo.)—Description
and travel. 5. Wyoming—Description and travel.   I. Title.
GT2346.U6.G75 2003
391.6'5'092—dc21   2003005603

Text set in Garamond MT
Designed by Cathy Riggs

Printed in the United States of America

First edition
A C E G I K J H F D B

for Sam, always

Skin Deep

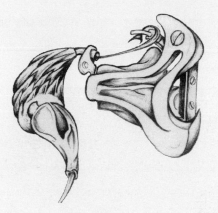

Prologue

First the skin is shaved, even if the hairs are few and baby fine. Clean the skin with an antiseptic soap solution. Wipe a folded paper towel across the top of a tube of deodorant and smooth a film across the skin. The deodorant makes the stencil image stick. The stencil is made by running a pencil drawing, sandwiched in a ditto master, through a thermofax machine. Peel off the gummy backing and press the flimsy paper, with its purple-line design, against the deodorant-coated skin. Tear open a packet of autoclave tubing, remove the needles, remove the tube. Fasten the tube into the machine. A tattoo machine is ingeniously simple, nothing more than a couple of electrical coils, a capacitor, and just enough power to push needles through skin. Rubber bands hold the needlebar in place, keep the needles from jumping up and down. Attach an electric clip cord to the machine, press the foot pedal, and adjust the rheostat on the power pack until the speed of the stroke is just right. Wipe a smear of petroleum jelly along the stencil line and stretch the skin with a latex-gloved hand, leaning into the body with a pressure that is both comforting and intimidating.

You have to sit still.

Dip the needles into a tiny cup of black ink; press the foot pedal as the machine is lowered to the skin. Carve the needles along the stenciled line, wiping away the excess ink with a paper towel twisted between the fingers of the hand holding the machine. The skin gives slightly before the needles push through.

Dip, press, pierce. A thousand times a minute.

Shading and color. That's what happens next. A

gray wash is tattooed first, for dimension and shape. The colors are added from darkest to lightest, like a paint-by-number kit. Red here, blue there, yellow blending from orange to green.

The skin begins to rise, and tiny blood bubbles pulse to the surface of the freshly tattooed mark. Angry red welts make the tattooed skin multidimensional, and it's hard to believe that it will ever feel normal again. Depending on the size of the tattoo, it might take twenty minutes or multiple sittings of several hours each to complete the work. No matter how long the tattoo takes, this time is only a tiny fraction of how long the tattoo will last.

"YOU LOOK," Savic says, "like a knocked-up hillbilly."

I am wearing green socks, combat boots, a black sweater that hangs funny, and a pinkish brocade dress that is ankle length in the back and barely reaches to my knees in the front. Seven months pregnant. When I cross my arms over the wriggling mound that is both me and not me, tattoos shoot out from my sleeves. This looks contradictory somehow, and I find myself wondering about the absent father and his tattooed arms, which are both like and not like my own. I wonder if he thinks of me when he looks at my artwork on his arms, or if he only thinks of me when he cracks his knuckles before curling his hands into fists.

Savic looks out the door of the tattoo shop at the snow blowing sideways across the parking lot, takes a long drag on his cigarette, and closes his eyes like he's getting ready for something big. "Picture it," he says. "I'm a traveling salesman and you're standing on a porch in that outfit with a bottle of 'shine in one hand and a little black dog tucked under your arm. As I'm walking up the lane, you say, 'Sho' is hot today.'" Savic's falsetto Appalachian impersonation fades away, and he is smiling to himself.

"Savic!" Karen looks like an angel, her beautiful face framed by cotton-candy pink hair. She's not mad at him, just concerned that her husband will offend someone, which he sometimes does, but usually unintentionally. I don't take his daily forays into weird sex fantasies seriously. They're more outrageous than obscene. But Karen worries.

"What's the dog for?" I ask. Savic just grins and lights another cigarette.

Savic is my boss at Zowie Tattoo, and I adore him,

even though he is the tiniest bit scary, a whole lot moody, and prone to verbalizing lurid thoughts. His usual work uniform is this: black leather pants, a red lamé shirt, and a black leather Confederate cap with sunglasses clamped above the brim. He is from Georgia, and everyone in Wyoming who isn't wearing Wrangler jeans and a cowboy hat looks like a hillbilly of one sort or another. It's the opposite of an insult, seeing as how Savic comes from hillbilly stock himself. It's just that Wyoming isn't quite what he expected.

Shortly before Zowie Tattoo opened, the shop was burglarized. The burglars took everything—the designs off the walls, the machines, needles, ink. Zowie was the third tattoo shop to be burglarized in Laramie in as many months, and the police didn't seem to be taking this sort of crime very seriously. Savic and Karen were determined to open the shop, no matter what. They used up the last of their savings to replace the stolen equipment, and tattoo artists across the country contributed whatever they could. Business has been good, but not good enough. The shop rent is exorbitant, especially for a gas-station-turned-office-space in desperate need of environmental remediation. The shop resonates with Savic's plaintive mantra—*I just want to draw pictures on people*—which doesn't seem like too much to ask.

I knew who Savic was long before he arrived. Pick up almost any tattoo magazine, and you'll see his work. I met with Savic and Karen at the Buckhorn Bar a month before they moved west. Sure, we agreed, Laramie had lots of turnover and plenty of clients. It would be a great place for a new tattoo shop. My portfolio had been lost somewhere, so I spread out my meager collection of loose photos on a sticky bar table. Savic nodded approvingly.

"Why'd you quit?" he asked.

"The first time, I got married and moved to San Francisco. The second time—" There weren't really words to explain it, but Savic and Karen were looking at me expectantly. I left out the part about the absent father and chose a reason that was less personal and easier to articulate. "There's this guy who works at Mini Mart," I said. "His face has been pierced so many times that it looks as though he's had an unfortunate encounter with a Slinky. And he's got a Maori moko design tattooed on his chin."

"And?" Savic looked puzzled.

"He's co-opted a culture he knows nothing about," I said. "Plus, too, he's got a tattoo right in the middle of his face, but he looks somehow confused about why he's working the graveyard shift at a convenience store. I got tired of contributing to other people's lapses of judgment."

SAVIC AND KAREN aren't the only new folks in town. People are moving here in record numbers, tossing around city phrases like "quality of life" and "eco-tourism." They come here hoping to escape their pasts—the crime, the pollution, and the inflated economies of urban areas—but they're looking for the West that exists more in myth than in reality. They settle in cul-de-sac arrangements of expensive city houses in subdivisions with names like "The Buttes" and "Antelope Ridge," which are the only western things about them. They see the possibility of inventing new, fruitful lives, but when this doesn't happen, or at least doesn't happen easily, they become overpowered by the need for a three-dollar mocha latte. That's how it started. A coffeehouse here, a chain music store there. A subdivision on the top of the rolling hills east of Laramie, once a sacred Indian burial site. Consultants and telecommuters

now outnumber ranchers and miners. Like Savic and
Karen, they've all come here to settle the frontier West.
The funny part is that I've never thought of Wyoming
as a frontier. A frontier is someplace you go; this is
where I live.

Zowie is on the corner of Second Street and
Custer, on the fringe of downtown Laramie. It's a
downtown that looks nothing like it did twenty years
ago. It is still Laramie, there's no mistake about that,
but it feels like a colorized movie, looks somehow
computer-enhanced. Galleries and gift shops have replaced the hardware, drug, and five-and-dime stores as
part of a western gentrification conducted by newcomers who are better off, better educated, and more determined in their concentrated fervor to carve out a

place in the wilderness than the people for whom Laramie has always been home. Instead of guns and cavalry, these newcomers have conducted their unintentional crimes of conquest and dispossession with technology and economics.

Downtown Laramie has become charming, more welcoming and more western than it has been for nearly a century. New streetlights, made to look old, shine above wooden benches and replicas of barrel halves filled with blooming foliage in front of more than a few storefronts filled with western art and artifacts behind gleaming glass, price tags tastefully turned facedown.

As downtown Laramie changed, the scales tipped slowly from function to form. Function was relocated to the eastern side of town, a flood zone littered with car dealerships, fast-food restaurants, and Wal-Mart, all of which were more generic than western. The eastern edge of Laramie could have been grafted from any other smallish city in America. The convenience of national brands and discount prices is as familiar as someone else's hometown on a television show, which suggests a bit of backpedaling about what, exactly, city people had wanted to escape when they moved to the West.

At the same time, tattoos became less about cultural authenticity and more about possession. Tattooing seemed to have become a commodity of coolness, and speed was of the essence, a fast-food version of body modification.

It wouldn't seem they'd have much in common, a geographic region and a permanent mark on the skin, and if it weren't for the coincidence of hometown and career, I wouldn't have noticed any connection between tattooing and the West. But there I was, western and tattooing, when both place and mark became more desirable, not for what each one was, but for what each one had been or could become. There was no present tense.

It wasn't as though anyone organized a group or drafted an army of invaders. The changes in the West and tattooing all began as individual paths aiming for some sort of self-improvement, but these paths had a tendency to converge whenever people started comparing notes about what they hoped to find. The West and tattooing were both mapped out, person by person, a collective topography of individual desire.

I'M SITTING IN the front room at Zowie. Savic's machine is buzzing away in the distance while I wait for the next customer and flip through a tattoo magazine, not really reading. I'm trying to decide what to tell the wriggle in my belly about its father, even though I figure I've got a good five years before it starts asking questions. Song lyrics spring to mind, pushing aside more practical explanations. *He was a hardheaded man/He was brutally handsome/She was terminally pretty.* What he sang while we eluded a police chase last May. Life in the fast lane, and I love to drive. *He was the ghost of a Texas ladies' man.* What he sang in bed, naked and sweaty after the lights were out. *Wherefore art thou Romeo/You son of a bitch.*

A few months ago, the absent father was busted, extradited, heard in court. Now he's just waiting to be sentenced, but somewhere between extradition and court he decided I must have been the person who tipped off the cops. At least that's what he said while he was beating the shit out of me and his unborn child. I didn't fight back, didn't do anything. I just stood there, unable to raise my hands high enough to protect anything more than the baby, frozen in disbelief because his weapons were decorated with my tattoos. He picked me up by the neck and slammed me into the side of my car. When that wasn't enough to make me cry, he pulled out a .357 Magnum.

I cried then, begged for my life. For my child.

An unspoken western code governs honor among outlaws, which is why I didn't press charges. That, and fear. Breaking up, though, seemed like a very good idea.

I DECIDE TO STOP thinking about the absent father. I walk next door to the pool hall and buy a package of stale Slim Jims from the vending machine. Before I got pregnant, I didn't eat meat, mostly because I like the looks of cow faces. Plus, too, I thought it was hypocritical to eat a formerly living creature if I would not have the courage to kill it myself. Now I crave protein, especially beef. Rare steaks and huge hamburgers and ropy sticks of jerky. I eat with no remorse, even though I still lack the mettle to kill.

Tattooing at Zowie is my second job, and it seems like I'm always tired. I wonder if I should quit my day job and tattoo full time, but then I'd lose my health insurance, so I work seven days a week instead. Seven A.M. till four P.M., hiding my tattoos and making photocopies. Four P.M. till eleven P.M., sleeves pushed up and pushing ink. Two jobs, fourteen-hour days. I didn't think I'd ever work in a tattoo shop again, but I also didn't expect to be pregnant, pregnant alone. At night,

I leave Zowie in a hurry for a shower. I tuck away my tattoo money, which has become baby money. After I wash off the smell of cigarettes and antibacterial soap, I lie on the couch, exhausted but unable to sleep. I watch Lifetime: Television for Women, lots of made-for-TV movies about abused women who eventually turn on the men who terrorized them. Sometimes I clap. Mostly I just lie on the couch, touching my belly and eating meat.

"Can I help you?" I smile at the three young men when they come through the door. One of them steps forward as though volunteering for an odious mission.

"Yeah." He sniffs and snorts in a manly sort of way and hitches at the crotch of his pants. "I want a tattoo." He scans the flash on the first wall and thunks a stubby finger repeatedly against a tiny Superman symbol. "How much?"

"Forty dollars."

"Let's do it." He looks to his companions for approval and the front room hums with a wave of vicarious excitement. I pull the flash sheet off the wall and trace the design. "I want it in red and black, though," he says, breathing on me while I sharpen my pencil. "No yellow."

"No problem." I hold up the tracing paper. "I just need to make a stencil and we can get started."

"I don't want the S in it," he says as though I should have known better. "I want a D."

"D?"

"My name's Dave," he says. I erase the S and try to draw a satisfactory D inside the triangle. The tracing paper is gray and littered with eraser rubbings before I decide to call it quits.

"The only reason this symbol works graphically is because of the S. The D doesn't work," I say, surveying my efforts. "Maybe if it's a lowercase D—" I redraw it one more time and hold it up.

He shakes his head. "I don't want a little D. I don't want to be Little Dave."

"You don't seem to mind being Duperman," I mutter, erasing until the paper rips. Eventually the big D is awkwardly placed in the center of the triangle, and Duperman approves it after conferring with his friends.

I belly up to Duperman, stretching his skin with my right hand and tattooing with my left. I've seen really fat tattoo artists, and I'm wondering how they manage. My elbows are lodged in the top of my stomach, and I'm anything but comfortable. Without warning, the baby kicks furiously. I lose the stretch on Duperman's arm, and even though I pull the tattoo machine back, the needles snag the skin. Duperman doesn't notice, but Savic does. I look down at the wide place this mistake has left in an otherwise perfect outline and look up at Savic with dismay. We both look at my belly; I can't tattoo much longer.

𝒶 GAY UNIVERSITY of Wyoming student is brutally beaten, tied to a pole fence. Dies. This makes national headlines and causes local businesses to post signs: VI-OLENCE IS NOT A LARAMIE VALUE. Media people swarm through town, interviewing anyone who will stand still in front of a camera or tape recorder. We all agree it's a tragedy. A week later I hear my own voice on NPR, a sound bite from a barely remembered interview. Thirty minutes answering questions into a tape recorder in Zowie's waiting room, and all that airs is this: *Violence is, too, a Laramie value.* What they left out was the part about Laramie's past, about the vigilante lynchings from streetlamps and the trees lining Grand Avenue. They left out the part about how, now, women are the victims of western violence most of the time, women whose bodies are dumped out in Rogers Canyon or along Happy Jack Road, and how this usually rates only a small local newspaper article, not national coverage.

The media's indictment of Laramie as a whole for Matthew Shepard's murder causes many of the people who'd moved here from other places, the people who'd renovated and gentrified old houses and our downtown, to distance themselves from what they'd created, like Dr. Frankenstein refusing responsibility for his monster.

"We moved to Laramie _____ years ago from _____ *(Fill in the blanks with any number and city)*, and we are shocked *(stunned, outraged, sickened, appalled)*. This is the last place we'd have expected something like this to happen *(This isn't our Laramie)*." Every time people who've moved here from somewhere else are interviewed about this murder, some permutation of this sentence is slipped in, excusing their gullibility as much as anything else.

Wyoming is supposed to be inhabited by men with weapons and callused knuckles; it's one of the things that makes the West so western. Western violence is excused—even admired—because it is part of a romantic myth. Those who move here from other places half expect a quaint bunch of "When you call me that, smile" gun-toting cowboys ready to risk a life over words, but in this fantasy, the guns are, of course, not pointed at them.

Savic has taken to accessorizing with a shoulder holster and semiautomatic handgun. Karen looks pinched. Business is slow, and we are all worried about money, burglars, killers.

A chest-high counter, a half circle with a black lacquer top, takes up nearly half of Zowie's waiting room. The sides are covered in a metallic collage of retro shapes that shift like holograms depending upon the angle. The counter is maybe two feet deep and hollow underneath, plenty of room for Savic's music collection, coats and purses, reference material, and custom tattoo designs in various stages of completion. The top of the counter is where we keep the appointment book and release forms. It's where we draw while we wait.

A week ago, I was standing behind the counter, putting a release form on the clipboard for my next appointment, when two men came into the shop. They both had mustaches and were wearing badges on their belts. They both smelled like cop.

"Are you Karol?" The taller one asked.

"Yeah."

He nodded slowly and sucked his teeth, as though just being me was evidence of some sort of wrongdoing.

"What can I do for you?" I asked. I wasn't especially surprised to see them. The absent father and I had done a few things that might warrant their presence; I just wondered which thing, specifically, they might be here to inquire about.

"I'm Detective Schiff," the taller one said. "This is Detective Benson. We'd like to ask you some questions."

"Okay," I said. I rested my elbows on the counter and waited.

"Actually," Detective Benson said, "we'd like you to come with us. To the police station."

"For questioning," Detective Schiff added.

"I've got an appointment in ten minutes," I said. "But I could pop by later, like around three o'clock, if you want."

Detective Schiff's brow furrowed. "You can't just 'pop by' for questioning," he said. "This is a very serious matter."

"You're under suspicion," Detective Benson said.

"Suspicion of what?" I asked.

"We'll ask the questions," Schiff said. "Now you can either quit stalling and come with us, or I can arrest you right now."

"Your choice," Benson said.

"Okay." I reached under the counter for my purse, and Detective Benson grabbed the leather strap before I could swing it over my shoulder.

"I'll take that," he said, and yanked my purse hard across the lacquered surface.

I walked around the counter. I was halfway to the door when I realized that the officers hadn't moved. They were standing right where they'd been, like slack-jawed statues. Detective Benson was holding my purse, and both sets of detective eyes were pinned on my belly.

"You coming or what?" I asked.

"Actually, it seems that our information may have been less than accurate," Schiff said. "Could we talk privately here somewhere?"

Benson put my purse on the counter and we went into my tattoo booth. Schiff closed the door. He sat down on my stool and I sat on the edge of the massage table Savic liked to use for backs and legs. Benson just stood there, staring at my belly.

"We received a tip," Schiff said, "that you were responsible for burglarizing a bistro last weekend."

"A bistro? I don't think I've ever heard anyone say 'bistro' out loud," I said.

"The perpetrator," Schiff began.

"Or perpetrators," Benson interrupted.

"Broke a small pane out of a skylight in the roof and rappelled into the structure." Schiff nodded as though he'd explained everything. There was a long pause.

"Hmm," I said, hoping to spur the conversation forward.

"No offense," Schiff said, "but there's no way you could have fit through the opening."

"Why would someone try to pin something like this on you?" Benson asked.

"Can I play 'guess the snitch'?" I said the absent father's full name out loud, resisting the urge to clean my tongue with my sleeve afterwards.

"Yeah," Schiff said. "He's trying to stay out of prison by giving people up."

"Rumor has it that he beat up his girlfriend," Benson said. "Would that be you?"

"I guess," I said, "but from what I hear, there could be others."

"It's a bit of a shock to find out he lied about you," Benson said. "I wonder if any of the other cases he gave us are bad."

"Why would he nark you out for the bistro burglary," Schiff asked, "when it's obvious that you're way too big—"

I gave him a look, mostly for the comment about my size, but partly for saying "bistro" again.

"He means way too pregnant big, not that you're big otherwise," Benson said.

"He thinks I turned him in because of something a cop told him," I said, "plus he suffers from a chronic lack of foresight and hasn't seen me for a few months. No way of knowing I look like this now."

"It'd really help us out," Benson said, "if you'd testify at his sentencing hearing." He went on and on about how helpful I could be. Any testimony would do, it seemed. I could tattle about the felonies they suspected the absent father of committing, or I could tell the judge about the day I thought he was going to kill me. Anything to ensure he'd have to serve the sentence he had hanging over his head.

"We can charge him with attempted murder for what he did to you," Schiff said. "It'll never stick, but he'll definitely do at least eighteen."

"Years?" I asked.

"Months."

"I don't think so," I said. As far as I could tell, that would just give him a year and a half to work himself into an indignant rage, a year and a half to figure out how to kill me properly.

"Aiding and abetting," Benson said. "Harboring a fugitive, eluding police, resisting arrest." One finger at a time, he ticked off the crimes with which I could be charged if I didn't cooperate and testify like a nice girl. They were misdemeanors, mostly, so I shrugged.

"I don't have any sort of record," I said. "Even if those stick, I won't do any time."

"You think you have a working knowledge of criminal law, huh?" Schiff leaned back and gave me a condescending smile.

"I'm not trying to be difficult," I said. "I just don't want to be dead."

"During John's trial, he got up on the stand and said that he shouldn't go to jail because he's got a kid on the way and he needs to support it." Benson pointed at my ever-expanding belly. "I'm assuming he was talking about that."

"I guess, but from what I hear, there could be others," I said again.

"Have you gotten any support from him?" Schiff asked.

"He sent me a package of diapers and a bib that says 'Daddy loves me' the day after he beat me up," I said. "He never did have much of a sense of irony."

GROWING UP WESTERN made it easy to become tattooed at a time when tattoos weren't especially popular. I'd gotten a good dose of the importance of expressing one's individuality at an early age, and I bought into the romantic myth of tattoos as a mark of the outlaw. I lived for a time in a tattooed West, and I was happy there, but it was the kind of taken-for-granted happiness that sneaks out of your heart before you know it's gone. I stayed West and kept tattooing, just in case it was the kind of happiness that might wander home.

There's a world of difference between having a tattoo and being a tattooed person, just like there's a world of difference between living in the West and being a westerner. When I started getting tattooed, a sense of kinship seemed to knit tattooed people into a colorful community. This isn't true anymore. Maybe it's because MTV has planted the seeds of tattoo desire in the fallow soil of teenage minds from coast to coast. Maybe it's because I've seen so many people rush into tattoos with little thought for design, placement, or permanence. Maybe it's because some people use tattoos more to shock others than to please themselves. Whatever the reason, I've learned two things to be true. First, one tattoo does not a tattooed person make. Second, when I see someone with a tattoo on his face or neck, I know that he and I are tattooed for completely different reasons, and that this is only the beginning of the differences between us.

The only tattooed people with whom I feel an inky kinship are those who are fully sleeved — tattooed from shoulder to wrist—on both arms. This speaks of a shared commitment of time and pain and dedication to an art form. If nothing else, there's a flash of recognition and a nod of acknowledgment. Commitment and commonality breed a certain level of trust, however uneasy; full sleeves usually belong to bikers, felons, and other tattoo artists, at least in Wyoming.

Before Zowie, the last time I tattooed was in an abandoned storefront with boarded-up windows somewhere in southern Colorado. This was before I got pregnant, back when the absent father and I acted like we thought we were Bonnie and Clyde. We were on the run from the law. More accurately, he was on the run; I was just aiding and abetting. I tattooed both of his arms from shoulder to wrist, new work wrapping around jailhouse pieces and a haphazard caricature of Elvis. The NCIC wanted-fugitive report mentioned the Elvis tattoo, and the work I did was as much a disguise as anything. *People will see only fully tattooed arms,* his rationale went, *not individual pieces.* He let me tattoo whatever I wanted, wherever it would fit. I had a pretty good time and slung some nice ink, but by the time I finished, I was struck by the absurdity of tattoos as a disguise. This, after a thousand dollars' worth of tattoos in two weeks' time, power pack running off stolen electricity piped in through borrowed extension cords.

I think about some of the other things we did when he was on the run from the law, and I realize I could turn him in in a heartbeat. I know, though, that I won't, any more than one of the Wild Bunch would drop a dime on a former member of the gang.

I'M STANDING AT the sink in one of Zowie's two gas-station-style bathrooms, scrubbing my tubes with a wire brush. The autoclave bags are lined up on the counter, ready to be filled and sealed. I'm thinking about the cops, about Detective Benson specifically, the way he looked holding my purse. It had been stupid of me to pick it up in the first place; it's just that I'm used to hauling my purse around with me wherever I go. It's where I keep my money, my driver's license, my gun. That last thing is what would have gotten me in trouble. It's a revolver, loaded with hollow-point bullets and always within easy reach, but the detectives probably wouldn't have shared my opinion that not having a permit to carry a concealed weapon was the least of my worries. If it weren't for the baby, my life would have boiled down to the fact of that gun and fear tangled up with an unspeakable sadness, my .38 Special and my broken heart.

Karen pokes her pink-haired angel face around the doorway. "Phone call."

I put down the tube and the wire brush, go into the waiting room, and pick up the phone. I wish instantly that I hadn't. On the other end of the line is my once-upon-a-time favorite outlaw, the absent father. I had hoped I'd heard the last of him, but he disappoints me once again.

"How do you like it, huh?" It was a voice that used to make my heart beat faster, a throaty bass once capable of triggering glee or passion or both, but now my heart skips a beat and jumps into my throat. Fear. I cradle my belly protectively with the hand that's not holding the phone.

"Like what?" I ask.

"Getting arrested. Now you know how *I* feel, huh."

"I didn't get arrested," I say.

I notice two customers, Savic's last appointments of the day, pretending to be intent on the tattoo magazines, but their ears are pricked forward, toward the counter and my voice. I think about hanging up, but there's a part of me that secretly hopes for an apology, secretly wishes that the absent father was still the man I fell in love with instead of the man he'd become, even though I know that both are just parts of one person and that he was probably more bad than good to start with. I just don't want to be stupid for having trusted him. Don't want to be foolish for having loved him as long and hard as I had.

"I'm too pregnant to do what you told them I did," I say. "Simple physics."

"You think you're so fuckin' smart, huh? You're gonna force me to take action against you."

"Did you know that it's an automatic aggravated assault charge when you hit a pregnant woman?" I ask like it doesn't matter one way or another. "Even without a weapon." Idle conversation. "I think it's a felony if you just hurt a pregnant woman's feelings." This spawns a new set of threats, most of them violent and all of them vivid.

"Nobody's even gonna find the body when I'm done with you. Got any idea what a bullet can do to a person's insides when you shoot 'em in soft tissue?"

I put the receiver down gently on the counter and go back to scrubbing my tubes.

"You on the phone?" Savic comes in and leans against the doorjamb.

"Not really," I say.

"Did you know there's a screaming asshole on the other end?"

"Yeah."

"Is it your, um, the baby's, um—" Savic feels bad for me more often than he should. We don't talk about the absent father much. When we do, Savic ends up making lewd jokes and laughing a little too loud, just to take my mind off it.

"Yeah."

"He's really running his neck," Savic says. "Sounds kind of like Donald Duck from here."

I turn off the water and listen to the unintelligible squawking coming from the receiver.

"Fucking lunatic," Savic says. "I was going to call for pizza."

"Go ahead," I say. My tubes are clean and bagged and waiting in the autoclave. Savic will turn it on when he's done for the day. I follow him the few steps from the restroom to the waiting room and watch as he picks up the receiver and lets loose a belch into the mouthpiece, a belch so loudly impressive that the building seems to tremble. Savic holds out the silent receiver, looking pleased with himself, and presses the disconnect button.

I put on my coat and button the top three buttons, the only ones that still meet. The wriggle in my belly shifts. An elbow—or maybe a knee—becomes a visible lump through the fabric of my dress, and I rub it gently until the wriggle shifts again, into a more comfortable position.

Outside Zowie, I stand on the corner, waiting for the light to change, listening to the raucous laughter coming from the Fireside Tavern across the street and the rumbling of the eleven o'clock Union Pacific freight train a block away. The snow makes yellow halos

around the streetlights and collects in doorways and
along the curb.

"What has Wyoming come to," I ask the baby,
"when tattoos have lost all meaning and outlaws turn
out to be just bad men?"

Chapter One

WYOMING AND TATTOOING were "discovered" by white people at roughly the same time. Two thousand years ago, Wyoming was a place nomadic people traveled to when they needed bison for food or quartzite to make sharp things. The people who came here took what they needed and traveled on or went back to wherever they came from. Alkali ponds and fish fossils were the only souvenirs of Wyoming's prehistory, the epochs and eras during which most of the state had been covered by a saltwater lake that gradually dried up like affection soured.

Two thousand years ago, permanent body alteration, usually in the form of tattooing or scarification, was common in non-Western cultures, often done as a rite of passage from childhood to adulthood. Tattoos signified a person's character and status within a society. The process was painful and time-consuming, but attention spans were considerably longer then, distractions were markedly fewer. A tattoo could be made with anything sharp enough to break the skin—metal, if you had it, sharpened rock or serrated shell and bone if you didn't—and soot was usually the main ingredient in any pigment.

In 1769, Captain James Cook, an English explorer, brought home tales of the practice of "ta-tu" in Tahiti, and his stories were illustrated by some of the members of his crew who had gotten tattoos as souvenirs of their journey. To make this Tahitian mark, a narrow piece of wood inlaid with a series of fish bones was dipped into pigment, placed against the skin, and tapped with a rod held in the tattooist's other hand. On his second voyage to Tahiti, Captain Cook brought back a tattooed man called Omai, who evolved from tribal royalty to sideshow freak as he stepped ashore. Eventually, European sailors attached magical powers to tattooing; a pig tattoo on the top of one foot and a chicken tattoo on the top of the other were thought to be a charm against drowning. Instead of fish bones, needles bound to a piece of metal or wood were used to make the mark.

In America, Wyoming still wasn't a popular place, mostly because of its inhospitable climate and the distances between watering places. Bison fared better a few hundred miles to the east, and intertribal wars kept the human population down. There were fewer than ten thousand nomadic Native Americans inhabiting Wyoming when the white people showed up.

The United States has a history of losing its innocence and then forgetting all about what happened. The West wasn't America's only frontier; it wasn't even America's first. By the time Americans got around to the West, most of a continent had been purchased or conquered in a collie-wobble cadence of falling wilderness and rising settlements. In the early 1800s, explorers returned from the wilderness west of the Mississippi River with dreamy stories of landscapes unlike anything anyone had ever seen; the West was a real-life Garden of Eden, full of promise and sublime in the antiquated sense of the word. The West was America's first *last* frontier. There was a market for this.

The West was packaged like a presidential candidate and airbrushed into porn-star perfection. Its virtues were writ larger than life, and everything else was embellished, forgotten, or reinvented until the West became synonymous with easy money and self-fulfillment. It came complete with celebrity endorsements and the limited warranty of the Homestead Act. As frontiers went, this was *new!* And *improved!* And advertised around the world.

Surveyors traversed the Continental Divide in 1855, mapping out the path of the railroad tracks that would connect both coasts. The government gave the railroad twelve million acres along the route, compensation for laying the tracks that would undoubtedly lead to the fulfillment of Manifest Destiny—the decree, supposedly straight from God, that the United States had not only a right but a duty to expand across the continent. This expansion would

certainly culminate in the collective achievement of the
American Dream.

For the next fifty years or so, most Americans invested such hope in the romantic version of the West that,
when they saw it first hand, they refused to consider the
possibility that their expectations might be foiled by topography, climate, or the vagaries of weather. Even when
everything about the West turned out to be harsher than
advertised, it was idyllic in one way or another, seasonally
romantic, and more promising than already civilized places.
Most settlers stuck it out with the idea of making a better
life for their children, if not for themselves, combined
with religious beliefs that left little room for laziness or
giving up. The same faith painted death as a reward, and
probably it was, more often than not. Thinking of the future meant thinking of one's children and heaven, not necessarily in that order.

As the populations of frontier settlements grew, the
more ascetic pioneers moved on, the crybabies moved
back to civilization, and those who were left welcomed
their new, not-so-brave neighbors with barn raisings, baked
goods, and quilting bees. These new neighbors made
places for themselves on land that had been gentled but
not tamed. They took their time clearing roads, building
homes, and rotating crops; it was clear they weren't moving
on anytime soon.

BY THAT TIME, on the other side of the world, members
of Maori tribes in New Zealand augmented traditional

Oceanic tattoos with the art of moko, facial tattoos that were carved into the skin with chisels in a manner that left the freshly tattooed person eating through a funnel for quite some time. Every moko was unique, based upon the different contours of each face. Moko combined cultural meaning and individual self-expression for the first time in the history of tattooing.

Moko evolved from a symbol of social status into a symbol of economic success, until anyone who could afford to pay the tattoo artist could buy a moko. The painful and elaborate chiseling involved in the moko technique was unique to the Maori, and, because it more closely resembled their woodcarvings than the needle-poked tattoos with which they adorned themselves from the neck down, it was unique to tattooing.

While Maori tribes battled amongst themselves in the 1800s, enterprising Europeans took advantage of the Maori predilection for decapitating prisoners of war. The act of beheading was more important to the warring tribes than the pieces of people it created, and traders picked up souvenirs from both friend and foe. Tattooed Maori heads were smoked like hams and bartered like trading cards. The entrepreneurial gusto of the European collectors was matched by the tendency of some of the Maori to increase the value of their severed and smoked merchandise with the posthumous creation or enhancement of the mokos on their enemies' faces.

On another side of the world, Japanese tattooing could be traced back as far as tattooing in any tribal culture, with similar primitive geometrical marking and ritualistic importance, not to mention the function-over-form tattoos on the hands and faces of Japanese divers, which were intended to frighten large fish away. From there, Japanese tattooing grew into a punishment by the seventeenth century, with facial tattoos serving as irrefutable proof that someone had done something legally unforgivable.

A century later, respectable Japanese people had nothing to do with tattooing, nor did they have anything to do with those who traveled in such indecent circles. The discovery of a single, small tattoo carried with it the same immediate snubbing as the discovery of an entirely tattooed torso or more; a person was either tattooed or not tattooed, period. Some Japanese people, though, cared very little about respectability, and those who were tattooed weren't confined to particular designs or cultural rites. The rise in popularity of full-body tattoos was part art and part reaction to the injustice of government-sanctioned vanity once the emperor decreed that only members of royalty were permitted to wear ornate clothing. By the early 1800s, Japanese tattooing was usually a well-kept secret by both tattoo artists and those people who invested the three to five years necessary to acquire the now-traditional irezumi full-body tattoo.

In 1869, near the end of the Edo period, Europeans and Americans took an interest in Asia, and tattooing in Japan was officially forbidden with the efficient guilt of a hasty housecleaning before unexpected guests arrive.

THE TRANSCONTINENTAL railroad reached Wyoming in 1868, connecting the east coast with the west at the rate of ten or fifteen miles of track each day. The distance between settlements was calculated according to the ground an

engine could cover befoer its boilers ran out of steam. For
the first time, railroad construction preceded civilization,
an anticipation of need instead of a response. Once the
Union Pacific Railroad decided that Laramie City would be
the next stop on the line, the railroad began selling plotted
lots of prairie. Within a week, four hundred lots in Laramie
City were sold, and it wasn't long before five hundred
buildings had been constructed, some of them tents, some
of them log, none of them built to last.

Three months later, a community that was previously
nonexistent had swollen to five thousand people, most
of whom were gamblers, thieves, and prostitutes bent on
swindling the few law-abiding citizens.

WHILE LARAMIE CITY was experiencing its raucous begin-
nings, tattooists were opening professional shops in New
York and San Francisco. Laramie was nothing like these
urbane coastal cities. It was nothing like civilized. Laramie
was governed by a band of outlaws. Asa Moore was the
most notorious ne'er-do-well, proclaiming himself mayor
and ruling Laramie like a violent monarch with a twisted
sense of humor. No one was too good to die, his reasoning seemed to go, and he had a gang of henchmen ready
to back him up. He presided over the town from a canvas-
topped wooden saloon cheerfully referred to as the "Bucket
O' Blood." Wyoming was part of the Dakota Territory
then, but Laramie straightened up considerably when
Wyoming became a territory of its own. The more lawful
citizens of Laramie formed a vigilante mob and went after

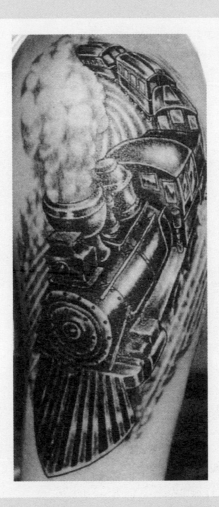

Asa Moore—soon to become the "late" mayor of Laramie—and his gang. They lynched whoever seemed in need of a good lynching and got a civilized hand on the politics in town.

When the railroad came through Wyoming, Chief Washakie's Shoshone tribe had agreed to move out of the path of civilization, onto the Wind River Reservation one hundred miles north of the tracks. Over the course of the next few years, most of Wyoming's other Native Americans were shunted off to reservations in neighboring territories. In 1878, the government decided to merge two previously warring tribes. They packed up the remaining members of the Northern Arapaho and moved them to Wind River to work out their differences with the Shoshone. Wyoming had only one reservation, which was something to be proud of then.

Wyoming became a state in 1890, the same year a New York tattooist, Samuel O'Reilly, was in the process of inventing the first electric tattoo machine, which he patented the following year. This machine was similar to one Thomas Edison had invented for an altogether different purpose, an electric stencil-maker used to punch holes in paper embroidery patterns. The industrialization of tattoo technology lessened the pain and time involved in the tattoo process and sparked an increase in popularity on both sides of the needle.

In the 1920s, Lew Alberts, a wallpaper maker, began reproducing sheets of tattoo designs (known as "flash") and selling them to tattoo parlors. Alberts is responsible for the traditional iconography of tattoo designs—hearts, flowers, animals, skulls, comic figures, dragons, images of religion and sex and allegiance to one group or another. During the 1920s and 1930s, tattooing was a common practice on both coasts, especially popular with soldiers and sailors; an article in a 1936 issue of *Life* magazine estimated that one in ten Americans had at least one tattoo. Interest in tattooing declined steadily after World War II, and by the time it was resurrected by bikers in the 1950s, tattooing was downright unpopular, which was why bikers liked it.

I was born in the 1960s, the same decade that spawned the Tattoo Renaissance. At the time, tattooing was still a marginalized activity, but educated artists who worked with other media were choosing skin for canvas, bringing a new sensibility to tattooing—more art than craft—and some of the people getting tattoos were interested in the possibilities of tattooing as an art form. The electric tattoo machine has remained virtually unchanged since its patent, but most every other technical element—especially pigments, flash, and sterilization procedures—were improving at a rapid pace. By 1970, tattoos had left the biker cliques and were heading for the mainstream, sometimes as art, sometimes for shock value.

In 1973, an Arab oil embargo tripled the average price of crude oil. Wyoming had more underground oil reserves than any other state, most of them located beneath rugged terrain owned by people who lived in other places. Before the oil embargo, the exertion of mining these reserves wasn't worth the effort, but in the 1970s Wyoming's resources were finally worth extracting. Mine shafts were dug, hill-sides were flayed open, and the earth inside was divided into what was valuable (which was hauled away) and what was not (which was left behind like a big wad of God's chewing gum).

$\mathcal{I}$ GREW UP IN a cheerful household in which setbacks were inevitably overcome, usually to the accompaniment of an upbeat, soaring, imaginary soundtrack. I grew up believing that more people were just like us than weren't, that the world was a kind place filled with honest people and forest animals who could speak. My mother and father fell in love at an early age. They both knew what they wanted and set out with an admirable and determined single-mindedness. My parents are stable and hardworking, the embodiment of the Protestant work ethic. They are the stuff of which the American Dream was made two generations ago. They set high standards and achieve them, realistic goal by real-istic goal. They are the sort of diligent people who instill responsibility, propriety, and good manners in their chil-dren. They expect that their children will turn out to be re-spectable and very much like them, because that is part of the long-term plan.

Mrs. Purdy, my sixth-grade teacher, sent me off to jun-ior high school with a few words of advice to my parents. "Karol always roots for the underdog," she said. "It's bound to get her into trouble sooner or later." My parents weren't especially worried. I was twelve years old, and the only trouble I'd found so far was the heartache of bringing home stray animals and failed attempts at mending half-dead birds. However, an innate characteristic of the western sensibility is the appreciation of the outlaw, a romantic view that permits the elevation of criminals and eccentrics to hero status, so long as they adhere to a western code of honor and individual freedom. Growing up in Wyoming gave me a peculiar mindset when it came to underdogs and outlaws, and I rooted for them out of sheer appreciation of their exclusion from the mainstream.

Low-grade marijuana was $40 an ounce — "ditch-weed," we called it. Like the other pseudo-bohemian girls at Laramie High School in 1979, I bought it from a surly girl in gym class, paying for it with money earned from sporadic baby-sitting jobs. I kept to myself and kept up my grades, a hit-or-miss honor-roll stoner mindful of the cause/effect relationship of a regular paycheck and steady weed. I was fifteen years old.

Shelving books at the Albany County Public Library, after school and on Saturdays, was my first job. I'd like to say I was good at it. I'd like to say I did my best when it came to putting away the mountains of books that accumulated in the shelving area. But I was not good at it, even though I did well for the first week or so and never really gave up hope. I was assigned to nonfiction, true stories and how-to books housed in a dimly lit maze of rickety metal shelves in a basement that smelled musty and slightly dangerous. I immersed myself in the Dewey decimal system, determined to render numerical order from the chaos of the "to be shelved" tables.

Among the dusty spines of the 811s, I once found an unimposing volume with a cryptic title: *The Kandy-Kolored Tangerine-Flake Streamline Baby* by Tom Wolfe. I removed the book from its place on the shelf, replacing it with the book of Wollcott essays in my hand, the book I was supposed to put away, the book that did not, according to the laws of Mr. Dewey's decimals, belong in that slot. I sat down on a stool meant for reaching the top shelves and began reading.

The Kandy-Kolored Tangerine-Flake Streamline Baby was about girls with bouffant hairdos and tight capri pants and boys who wore cigarette-leg jeans and white T-shirts. It was about rock music and art. Specifically, it was about cars, hot rods and customized autos. Wolfe explained cars in terms I could relate to—freedom, style, sex, power, and motion—but mostly *art*. Dali, Picasso, Mondrian, Brancusi, baroque, abstract, rococo, modern. I had thought that cars were the realm of greasy boys, but here was a whole new look at the subject. Car guys were portrayed as artists, creative outlaws willing to starve and suffer in order to realize their particular visions.

It wasn't long before I was caught reading, reprimanded, and demoted to fiction, which was alphabetical by author, upstairs, and closely monitored by the cardpunchers at the circulation desk. Reading on the job was trickier, the only real challenge offered by my demotion from the intricacies of decimal classification to the predictability of A through Z. I snuck paragraphs whenever I could and read S. E. Hinton's *The Outsiders* all the way through on a Saturday shift. I fell in love with the characters, boys with names like Soda Pop and Darry who greased their hair and rumbled. These boys weren't bad, just misunderstood, and I felt like one of the Outsiders even though I knew I'd never be mistaken for a teenage Texan boy. The author's initials stood for Susan and something that didn't matter; S. E. was a girl, and she'd written the book at the age of seventeen. I was Susan all over inside, Susan, the girl-writer who loved boys like this enough to understand them instead of trying to make them into something else.

This was the beginning of the end of my bookshelving career. I read more than I shelved; the top shelf of my cart was filled with books that were ready to be put away, but the bottom rack was where I stashed books I wanted to read, and as often as not, they were books I'd taken off the shelves, fiction mixed with the car books, art books, and outlaw biographies that I'd spirited up from the basement.

Eventually, the library found someone else to put the books away. I still went to the library almost every day, still read as much as I could. I spent my junior year stoned, with my nose in a book, rethinking everything I'd ever been told. By the time I was seventeen, the combination of library books, ditchweed, and solitude had left me with a collection of steadfast beliefs, most of which had to do with the relationship between outlaws and other people.

Billy the Kid was more interesting than Pat Garrett. Butch
Cassidy and the Sundance Kid had more fun than Starsky
and Hutch. I would rather read about Frank and Jesse
James than watch Donnie and Marie Osmond on TV.
Goodness is often painfully dull, and outlaws almost al-
ways have something more exciting to do.

I graduated from high school with seemingly sensible
aspirations. College and art, art and college. Two years
later, after a whirlwind of changing majors, having taken
classes that counted only as electives, and no closer to a de-
gree than I'd been when I started, I dropped out to become
a photographer. I had the combination of technical expert-
ise and insight measured down to an f-stop, and believed
that the coupling of talent and desire couldn't help but pro-
duce a satisfying career.

I thought my father would be pleased with my choice
after the initial shock wore off. He was the one who taught
me my way around a darkroom in the first place, the one
who explained apertures and shutter speeds, depth of field
and parallax view. He could be unobtrusive to the point
of invisibility with a camera lens between his eye and the
world, and he had the kind of patience that made the difference between good photographs and art. It wasn't something that could be taught or learned, just an unconscious
display of serenity and an artist's stealth. He was the one
who reminded me to take things slowly, to creep in, low
down and close.

"Photography? There's no money in it." He shook his
head. "And too much risk."

"Yeah," I said, "but what if I'm good at it?"

"I had to make a choice," he said, "between graduate school and photography. I had a wife and two daughters." He shrugged, palms up, as though that was explanation enough.

In 1983, I moved from my parents' house into a tiny attic apartment, just enough room for a bed and a second-hand couch. A pervasive air of ancient arguments, melancholy disappointments, and other people's cooking hung low in the dusty air. The carpet was threadbare, stained and worn down to a dusty pad in a path in the hallway. I cleaned rich people's houses for a living, marveling at all their stuff, so much of it unnecessary. Most of them had moved to Laramie from other places, but they had more

western effluvia than any ranch I'd ever seen, and most of these decorations were brand-new and expensive, except for the bleached cattle skulls.

By the 1980s, the West, with its vast empty spaces and implicit, mythic promises, seemed to be one of the last places the American Dream had a chance of coming true. Even so, my photography career was subsidized by a succession of forgettable jobs involving hairnets, safety-orange clothing, or worse, and success seemed less like a possibility and more like a prayer whispered on the cusp of sleeping or a birthday-cake wish.

One of the families for whom I cleaned, the Wilsons, had moved to Laramie a few years earlier, and Wyoming seemed to be living up to their expectations. Mr. Wilson's car dealership had begun as a prefab shed in a gas-station parking lot and grown into a block-square showroom on the busiest street in town. The Wilsons' house sprawled across two lots, full of gaudy bathrooms with oval-shaped bathtubs, wet bars, entertainment centers, and walk-in closets bigger than my apartment. They had white carpet everywhere and three teenage boys who didn't have chores. Their boys could urinate in the general direction of the toilet, secure in the knowledge that I'd be by every Tuesday and Friday to mop the piss stains off the floor.

Mrs. Wilson spoke to me only once, the day she hired me. It was the same day workmen were constructing a Plexiglas gazebo around her hot tub in the backyard. We were standing on the patio, looking at the workers who struggled to raise Plexiglas against a spring breeze.

"Does the wind always blow like this?" she asked.

"Pretty much," I said, stepping aside to make room for a man with an armload of two-by-fours.

"It sounds like traffic on the freeway," she sighed. "It's so loud. Sometimes I can't even think."

"It's because you haven't learned to separate the sounds," the man with the wood said. "Once you do that, your thoughts take on the same rhythm. You might think differently, but at least you'll be thinking."

$\mathcal{I}$ WASN'T THE KIND of photographer whose pictures could accompany newspaper articles or advertising copy, and I had no desire to coax small children into smiling on cue. I was an artist. I wanted my photographs to hang in galleries and museums, not above the fireplace in someone's split-level ranch home. Photography was a magic trick, an illusion. It was about choosing a particular reality, deciding a particular truth. That was the art of it, to me anyway, and the fibbing involved didn't seem dishonest.

I manipulated images with lenses and lighting, making things look like people and people look like things. I photographed blown cushions in junked cars, the stuffing spilling forth through decayed fabric that, under the right lighting, looked like torn flesh. I covered nude models with clay, dusted them with baby powder, posed them like statues, and waited until the clay dried and cracked before I snapped the shutter. I explored abandoned buildings and the Wyoming landscape, searching out patterns of light and dark, intriguing juxtapositions of the natural and the man-made.

Eventually my photography was all about skin.

After I tired of picking up after rich folks, I worked as a waitress, a highway construction flagger, and a disgruntled temp. I spent an afternoon as a phone-sex operator before I was fired for laughing. One morning, I opened my mailbox and found a final notice from the phone company, my monthly allotment of food stamps, and a letter notifying me that I had been nominated for a mention in *Who's Who in American Women,* which said that I had to send twenty-five dollars to defray publishing costs. I threw away the phone bill, filled out the *Who's Who* form, and mailed it back, along with twenty-five dollars in food stamps.

This was not the way things were supposed to be going. I didn't have a backup plan, and it looked like I needed to think one up. Quick. I got into my car and drove west, turning onto the dirt road that led to the place I went when I needed to think hard. A few miles later, I pulled over next to a NO TRESPASSING sign in an unfenced field, climbed the locked gate of someone's summer home, and ran across the yard, ducking low under the barbed-wire fence on the other side. Then I was on the Forest Service side of the fence, public property. An old mining road wound up the side of the hill, nothing more than two ruts, overgrown with weeds. It disappeared from time to time in the underbrush, but I'd been here before the house and the trespassing warnings and the locked gate. I climbed for a mile or so, and the path leveled out and turned south. I crossed a shallow creek, and the trail ended abruptly in a tangle of windfall aspens. I picked my way across and emerged on the top of a massive slag heap with a breathtaking view of the valley. Part of the mountain had been blasted away, an angry slashing that left behind scarred layers of rock, like vivisection. The mountain was pitted with mine shafts, and the tailings had been piled on top of tailings on top of more tailings to form a slag heap that jutted from the side of the mountain, littered with rusty mining equipment and the rotting boards of forgotten buildings.

I sat down and listened to the wind howling through the aspen and pines behind me, sighing across the sage in the prairie below. It ebbed and flowed around the mound of shale, shuffled through my hair, and roared away. The wind plucked my thoughts away from the earth and brought them back in a slightly different form. I knew exactly what it would be like to be tossed among the clouds, looking down on the shadows and the mountain as the music of the wind spun me out and away from the hold of the earth.

I found myself thinking about the slag heap instead of photography. The pile of tailings upon which I was sitting was once part of the mountainside. The mine that created the slag—which I found strangely beautiful, but which amounted, essentially, to littering—had irreversibly altered this particular piece of Wyoming, and it felt like a natural piece of the landscape, but it wasn't, and it hadn't magically appeared all at once. It had begun with a single rock, building gradually into the barn-sized lump upon which I sat. Nothing in the West is really all-of-a-sudden; most changes are just sort of slow. Gradual.

George, the owner of the store where I bought my film and darkroom supplies, was a gentle, artistic person who loved photography and treated his employees like family. He'd asked me often enough if I'd like to work there. I picked up a big handful of tailings and let the flat rocks trickle through my fingers. Maybe it was time to take him up on his offer. Even if it wasn't exactly the career I had in mind, at least it was about photography.

Chapter Two

BEFORE THE 1980s, tattooing had never been especially popular in Wyoming. There was a shop in Cheyenne, a good one, supported mostly by the people stationed at Warren Air Force Base. Occasionally some ink-slinging entrepreneur would open a tattoo shop in one of the boom towns—usually Gillette or Rock Springs—but when the booms went bust and the migratory miners and oil riggers moved along, the tattoo shops went bust, too.

Westerners didn't need tattoos, at least not in the way that people in other places seemed to need them. People in Wyoming prided themselves on both individualism and self-sufficiency, so there was no need for a tattooed symbol to separate anyone from the crowd. Besides, there wasn't much of a crowd from which one might separate. Simply

by virtue of being raised here, westerners belonged to a society whose predecessors had almost completely erased the
people they'd displaced. Maybe it seemed somehow wrong
to appropriate even one more thing from someone else's
culture. Maybe Destiny had Manifested enough already.

In the past, anything from either coast had been slow
to reach Wyoming and was usually diluted by the time it
got here, but the relocation of so many people in so short
a time hastened the arrival of many things we didn't think
we needed before.

In 1985, Slade Fiero opened the Body Art Workshop
on Grand Avenue in the heart of downtown Laramie, next
door to the Vitamin Shoppe. By then, I'd spent more than
a year watching other people's film whir through a processor at Rainbow Photography, right across the street.

Slade was a cocky person with an omnipotent attitude
about his profession and few qualms about what might or
might not constitute a good business deal, sometimes trading tattoos for drugs or guns or stereo equipment. He em-
bodied almost every negative connotation of the tattooist,
all rolled into a stocky little package with a bushy mustache
and neatly manicured hair. Underneath, though, Slade was
soulful, an artist at heart.

The proprietor of the Vitamin Shoppe, Margaret,
deeply regretted Slade's choice of location. She tried to
get the other downtown businesses to force him out, and
when that didn't work, she was reduced to standing in her
doorway with crossed arms, shooting dirty looks at Slade
and his customers.

The tattoo shop had been there only a few months the day I looked over the Noritsu film processor and out the window as Slade parked his truck at the end of the block and sauntered down the street. He waved when he saw me, then ran across the street to the Vitamin Shoppe, sneaking around from the side of the building. He dropped his pants to the ankles, bent forward, and backed up until his flesh was pressed against the window glass. He looked over his shoulder at the havoc this caused inside the Vitamin Shoppe, and did a little hula rub to call even more attention to his tattooed butt.

By the time Margaret called the cops, Slade was at work in his shop. Two policemen went into the Body Art Workshop and escorted him outside, where he listened in feigned horror to Margaret's accusations. Her indignation gave way to rage when the policemen refused to arrest Slade because she couldn't say—for sure—that he was the culprit. She'd only seen the tattooed ass, and while she couldn't prove that it was Slade's, she insisted he was the only possible suspect. While both policemen agreed with the logic of this assumption and offered to trade a verbal warning for his confession, Slade refused to say whether or not his butt was tattooed. He said he'd give some thought to mooning the officers some other time, that he just wasn't in the mood at the moment, which meant that they'd need a search warrant if they wanted a peek in his pants.

That evening, Slade caught my eye as I walked past and waved me into the tattoo shop. I sat on the edge of a couch and he leaned back in a swivel chair next to a desk covered with scraps of tracing paper and ditto masters. The shop smelled like soap and cigarettes. The walls were covered with a scumble of tattoo designs, large sheets of paper covered with pictures, some in color and others in black and white. I tried to focus on the individual designs, but the total effect was overwhelming. *Somehow,* I thought, *people pick a single image and put it on their bodies forever.* How did they choose? The more I looked, the more the designs blended into one big picture, like so much wallpaper.

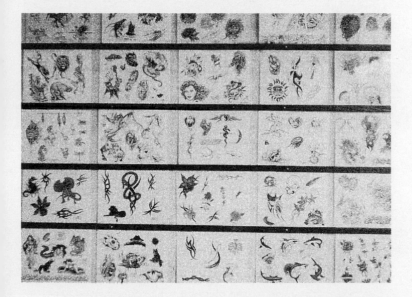

"So, what do you do?" Slade bounced a Camel Straight on the edge of the desk and looked at me expectantly.

"What do you mean?" I asked. "You know what I do. I develop film."

"Yeah, but what do you *do*?" He lit the cigarette and blew a succession of smoke rings toward the ceiling. "I always see you walking by yourself. Are you lonely? You got any friends?"

"Just because a person walks around alone doesn't make her lonely," I said.

"We'll hang out." It was decided.

I waited in the shop until closing time, studying Slade while he tattooed. He didn't look like a tattoo person. Slade was a short sturdy man with broad shoulders and chiseled forearms. His face was square, with luminous, girlish brown eyes fringed with dark lashes. A bushy mustache curtained his broad lips, and his eyebrows skittled across his forehead like two furry insects engaged in a tug-of-war over the bridge of his nose. His wide chin was beginning to show a faint trace of jowls, beginning as a deep furrow on either side of his nose, a ditch which plowed downward, skirting the mustache and disappearing into the stubble of his jaw where it pushed up two furry hillocks on either side of his chin. His wavy hair was blow-dried up and back from his high, square forehead, fluffed and shaped, gelled and spritzed into place. He was compact and muscular, with an extraordinary amount of conceit and energy coiled like a spring, waiting to explode all of his five-and-a-half feet. He was a classically handsome man with the rugged good looks of the Marlboro Man or Tom Selleck. He was confident, loud, and self-assured, and no one was more certain of his swarthy appeal than he was himself.

I watched as he worked his charm on the girl in the chair. She was a university student, a Native American woman from the Wind River Reservation, studying pre-law. She'd drawn her tattoo design herself, seven beads strung on leather, and each bead held a special significance, even though she wouldn't tell Slade what any of them meant. She'd drawn two eagle feathers where the band connected, and explained to Slade the details that made them eagle feathers; she said she wouldn't have him turning them into feathers that could have come from just any bird.

"Is this going to hurt?" Her voice was unemotional, but her foot shook in Slade's hand as he peeled the stencil away from her ankle.

"Well, let's see." Slade looked as though he were gearing up for an oft-repeated spiel. "You've got three needles here, poking into your skin about a thousand times a minute. Hell yes, it hurts." His eyes softened as he looked into her face. "No pain, no gain, sweetheart. You can do this. I know you can." He ran a gloved hand gently up the back of her calf. "Now just relax. That's it. You'll do fine." This reassurance was delivered with a lascivious caress, his fingertips lingering on the ball of her ankle.

When the tattoo was done and bandaged, she tipped him ten dollars and slipped him her phone number, and Slade gave her a hug as he opened the door. She looked back at him as she walked down the block, her eyes wide and moony above a big smile.

"God, I love my job," Slade said.

Slade lived in a converted garage, set back from the street behind his grandmother's house. The walls were lined with shelves filled with stuffed animals. A large television set took up the corner of the room. The twin-sized bed doubled as a couch, and the kitchen was part of the same room, a diminutive refrigerator, a tiny stove, and a small sink. We cooked dinner together and ate in front of the TV, talking about our lives and settling into a comfortable silence when we ran out of words. After we did the dishes, Slade stood on the bed, reached behind a blue teddy bear, and pulled out a bong.

"Made it in shop class in high school," he explained, as he cleaned the screen and loaded the bowl. He lit it, sucked in a huge hit, and held his breath as he passed the bong to me. I had a little bit, coughed, and immediately felt as though I needed to go to sleep.

Slade finished it off, and the sweet scent of pot smoke filled the room and hung in a haze in front of the TV. I struggled to focus my eyes on the images on the screen, but they no longer made any sense. I lay across the bed with my eyes shut while Slade flipped through the television channels and told me stories, undeterred by my lack of response.

"Stoned, huh?" He patted my back. "It's good weed. I got the best connections in town." He filled the bowl again and the water in the bottom of the pipe gurgled as he smoked. "I love weed. When I get stoned, I get horny and think about clothes. Yes ma'am. Basically, I turn into a teenage girl."

"You've certainly got the house for it," I said, and our laughter rose though the smoky room.

By THE TIME the Body Art Workshop celebrated its first anniversary, Slade and I had become best friends, the Vitamin Shoppe had moved down the block, Slade had expanded the tattoo shop into the other half of the building, and I'd learned that, if your best friend owns a tattoo shop, and you've got a camera, your artwork will eventually take a certain turn.

Slade stood in front of a black backdrop, fading into space. He had no qualms about stripping naked and posing for me, for my camera. The image was captured on film, and burnt momentarily into my retina.

I experimented with portraiture techniques, tricks of lighting and pose. When I ran out of color film, I switched to black-and-white. A few days later, I laid the contact sheets side by side. In color, Slade's personality faded away behind the tattoos, but in the black-and-white photographs, I saw Slade first.

I corralled as many tattooed people as I could find and photographed them in black-and-white. The resulting photographs transformed human emotion and tattooed flesh into art, with the lure of intimacy and honesty that ought to accompany both good portraits and sensual nudes. The negatives I chose to print were always the ones that made the strongest distinction between truth and appearance, between a chosen surface and the reality of the person inside.

I watched Slade tattoo a cobra on a man's shoulder, an ultra-realistic snake with a drop shadow beneath its head that made it look three-dimensional and alive, lunging off the skin. When the tattoo was almost finished, I introduced myself to Slade's customer and asked if he'd consider posing for a few photographs sometime.

"Sure," he said.

Slade explained my photographs to the man, Pete, while he worked, exaggerating a little bit about other people's interest in my work. "She's fucking incredible," Slade said. "Someday you're going to see books of her photos, and you're going to be able to say, 'Yeah, I knew her when…yeah, I posed for her, man, back before she was famous.'"

"Cool." Pete looked like he believed every word of it.

A week later, Pete plopped down a polyurethane cooler in the studio doorway. "You ain't afraid of snakes, are you?" He removed the cooler lid without waiting for an answer, and sank his hands into a writhing mass of multicolored scales. He lifted a snake with a gentleness I wouldn't have thought him capable of, clucking his tongue in the back of his throat and cradling the snake's body in his arms.

"This is Ruby." He raised the snake above his head and her body trickled through his hands toward his face. The snake stopped an inch above his nose, hovering. Pete tipped his head back and mimicked the snake's flickering tongue until the snake eased forward and tested his tongue with her own. They stayed that way, frozen except for their tongues, until the motor drive on my camera caught the snake's attention.

"Ruby's a reticulated Burmese python. Thirteen feet long." He wrapped the snake around his body and paraded around the studio as though he'd been posing like a movie star all his life. He danced with the snake, caressed it, let it curl around his tattoo. The closer shots were a mélange of scales and snake eyes, real and tattooed, blending together under the lights until you couldn't tell right away what was alive and what was ink. When I pulled the camera back, the image became a man and a snake entwined so sensually that it looked almost obscene.

After the film was gone, Pete eased the snake onto my arm. Ruby slithered up my shoulder and curved around the back of my neck, down the other side, squeezing and looking for warm places. My underarm, my crotch. The snake wound around my leg on her way to the floor. Pete picked her up and forced her mouth open. Two rows of curved, angry teeth gleamed beneath cold eyes.

"They can take a man's hand off," Pete said.

I should have known. Anything that felt so good was bound to have dangerous teeth. I looked at the snake as it curled around Pete's waist.

"Can I do it again?" I asked.

For the next few weeks, Pete spent most of his free time at the shop, explaining the process of tattooing to Slade's potential customers and describing his own experience to the uninitiated in painstaking detail. Anyone who didn't know better would have thought that Pete and Slade went way back, at least the way Pete told it, that theirs was a Rock of Gibraltar friendship growing stronger every day. Slade let it slide. Pete was decent company; he had a repertoire of good jokes, and he got all puffed up anytime he was invited past the "keep out" doors that separated the waiting room and the customers from the rest of the shop. His face lit up every time Slade said, "Hey man, c'mon back," smiling like a little boy with not much to look forward to or be proud of, the misfit kid from everybody's first-grade class who can't believe he finally got the answer right.

Pete wasn't alone. Some of Slade's customers would pay up, say their good-byes, and disappear forever, but others stopped by to ask Slade if their tattoos were healing properly, stopped by just to say hey, stopped by for no reason at all, propelled by a current of misplaced affection. If Slade was in the mood for a new friend or a change of face, he didn't mind. Sometimes he even felt that tattooing someone was a kind of fate, that he was destined to meet a particular person, and that such an encounter would never have happened had he not been a tattoo artist at the precise moment this person wanted a tattoo. Most of Slade's newly tattooed, new friends drifted away sooner or later, with some absences unnoticed, others unlamented, and a few greatly celebrated, but sometimes Slade was sorely disappointed. The newly tattooed new lover(s), the light(s) of his life, lost interest more than once as soon as the memory of getting the tattoo faded away. The newly tattooed best new guy friend(s), the one(s) who'd seemed to want nothing more than to spend every waking moment in Slade's company, the one(s) who'd offered up drugs or guns or girlfriends for that privilege, faded away, too, sooner or later.

It was the gloves, I thought, the latex gloves he wore when he tattooed. Every customer felt the unexpected excitement of a stranger's reassuring touch, and this one-sided intimacy transformed the gloves into the same kind of nothingness as a condom memento after a one-night stand. Slade tattooed four people a day on average, sometimes more, and their side of the experience meant undergoing a painful process with permanent consequences— for the first time, most of them—causing a tempest of emotions. Excitement and apprehension tangled with trust and physical discomfort and the adrenaline novelty of it all. Slade tattooed with his left hand and stretched with his right, a hand that looked like comfort and felt like something private, palm firm and flat against the body.

Some of them had to come back.

Occasionally, like Pete, after having been mourned, scorned, despised, or forgotten, they'd pop up unexpectedly with late-night, last-minute pleas for bail bonds or gas money. Collect calls, mostly, from people with nowhere to turn in a cul-de-sac of woes until they looked down at a faded tattoo and remembered the good times—and the tattoo-shop telephone number.

And then there were a few fleeting friends Slade wished he'd known longer, those who passed through like whitewater rapids instead of drifting by. In between missing them and wondering where a particular tattoo might have gone off to, these ephemeral friendships wove themselves into exuberant remember-when stories, like Cassie and Ray. These are the kind of memories you wish you had pictures of, just to remind yourself that real friendship is not the same thing as a fleeting reciprocation of impulsive attachment.

Ray and Cassie were the happiest people I'd ever met, even though, on the surface, it didn't look like they had much to be happy about. In fact, they didn't have much at all. But when Ray's motorcycle broke down in Laramie on the way to the Black Hills Bike Rally in Sturgis, and he found out that it would take almost a week to get the needed parts, Ray and Cassie cheerfully checked into a motel. Then they decided to check out the tattoo shop, which is where I met them.

They came in smiling. Ray's arm was draped proprietarily around Cassie's shoulders, and her arm was wrapped around his. Ray was wearing a Harley-Davidson T-shirt under a leather vest, and his boots jingled when he walked. He was a big man, and tall, with a neatly plaited braid that brushed his elbows and a salt-and-pepper beard. Ray looked like he was at least fifty, and Cassie was less than half his age. Her long hair was dyed blonde and all wadded up on top of her head. She was wearing a leather bikini top and faded jeans slung low. She was skinny, with no hips to speak of, and not especially pretty. But the instant she looked up at Ray and smiled, she became beautiful.

Slade and Ray looked like they were sizing each other up as they exchanged an unsmiling chin-lift that passed for a greeting. Slade introduced himself and me.

"I'm Ray," Ray said. "And this is my old lady."

Slade and Ray shook hands, and the talk turned to business.

"Hey," I said. "She's got to have a name."

Slade looked confused and Ray looked like he was thinking about getting mad. Then Cassie laughed.

"Cassie," she said. "My name is Cassie."

Ray began to chuckle. "Y'all are all right," he said.

An hour later, Ray was shirtless in the tattoo chair and Slade was working intently on a cover-up. Most of Ray's chest was covered with a series of hearts and the names of his ex-wife and kids inside a banner that switched back and forth like a mountain road. Slade had drawn an elaborate bouquet of flowers that obliterated the ex-wife's name, had given the lead edge of the banner a new beginning.

Ray's arms were completely sleeved with tattoos, and his chest and back were almost covered, too. I could tell from the styles and designs and the outline hues that ranged from broken-up blue to true black that he'd been getting tattooed longer than Cassie had been alive. His tattoos reminded me of old-fashioned hotel stickers on a steamer trunk, a record of where he'd been and what he'd done, in no particular order. Ray said that he got tattooed at Sturgis every single year, the size of the tattoo proportionate to his vacation fund. And every year for the past thirty, he'd also gotten a small commemorative tattoo, each one different, but all involving a banner with "Sturgis" and the year.

When the cover-up was done and bandaged, Ray and Cassie hung around for a few hours. They didn't have

anywhere to go, and we were all having a good time. Slade
got them talking, and it turned out that Cassie waited
tables and Ray worked with his hands, odd jobs and construction, mostly. His Harley had cost more than the
trailer they lived in, and they saved their money all year for
their annual pilgrimage to Sturgis. If they couldn't get time
off, they'd quit whatever jobs they had and worry about
getting new ones later. They both smiled big when they
talked about the bike.

The insecurity of it all made me wince and worry for
them. Ray noticed. Still smiling big, he held out his arm
and pointed to three faded blue-black letters. FTW.

"Fuck the world," he said. "You only got the one life,
so you gotta do the things that'll make you happy and blow
off the rest."

Ray and Cassie were back the next day. Slade tattooed
Thumper, the Disney rabbit from *Bambi,* big eyes and a
bunny smile, high on Cassie's hip, with rabbit footprints
that tracked back to the crack of her ass. We laughed all
evening about that, and Cassie's bandage crackled every
time she sat down.

They were back the next day, too. And the next. They
spent most of their vacation money on tattoos and bike re-
pairs, but Ray said it was cool. Didn't even mind missing
Sturgis that year, he was having so much fun. Besides, tattoo prices at the bike rally were more than double what
they were in any shop, and by the third day, Slade was
charging Ray and Cassie more out of principle than business. He would have tattooed them for free by the end of

the week, but Ray would have wanted to pay. Every night, Ray and Cassie left the shop with fresh ink and bandages on one body part or another.

One afternoon, Slade went down to the motorcycle shop with his camera. He photographed Ray's bike from every angle, and I developed the film in less than an hour. He spent an afternoon drawing and an evening tattooing Ray. The finished tattoo didn't look much like the photographs; it wasn't a flat representation of a motorcycle that could have belonged to anyone. Slade had created an animalistic foreshortened view of the bike that captured the way Ray felt about his Harley.

On their last night in Laramie, Ray and Cassie showed up with a fifth of Jack Daniels and a twelve-pack of Budweiser on ice. With the shop closed and the doors locked, Ray's last Laramie tattoo turned into a party that lasted until the sun came up. You shouldn't drink before you get tattooed, everyone knows that. It thins the blood, blurs your judgment. And having a sober tattoo artist also seems more than a little prudent. But sometimes you've got to make an exception, and a celebration combined with tattooing becomes a ritual all its own. We'd all become friends, and everybody would have some stories to tell.

In the morning, after lots of hand-shaking and hugging, Ray and Cassie climbed onto their motorcycle and waved good-bye. Cassie's arms were wrapped around Ray's waist, and she was smiling big, her chin on his shoulder, and the breeze knitted her hair with his as they rode away. Beneath the bandage on the underside of Ray's left arm

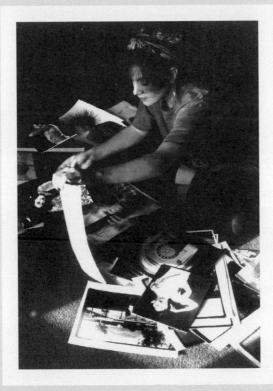

was a bouquet of Indian Paintbrush, Wyoming's state flower, and a banner that said "Sturgis '86." Underneath the banner, in parentheses, in Slade's best tattoo script, was the word "almost."

$\mathcal{L}$ARAMIE WAS ACCUSTOMED to a trickle of newcomers, people from other places who were determined to put their roots down here. The trickle turned into a stream in the late 1970s, and by the time the Body Art Workshop celebrated its second anniversary in 1987, the stream had grown into a river of city people looking for a better life. Everything in Wyoming, especially land, was relatively inexpensive, and the wind-thinned air and harsh landscape seemed full of promise and opportunity, as though this could be a place of forgiveness, a place where second (or third) chances might come easy.

I could see why they liked it here. Laramie didn't have that hungry-coyote look, that sparse and dusty feeling of some western places. Even though Laramie was all straight lines and right angles, there was a loose and unforced feeling about it, a sense of stability and optimism, along with a mischievous air that hinted at its wild and wicked roots.

The newcomers bought old houses and fixed them up. They built new neighborhoods and revitalized downtown Laramie. The furniture store burned down, taking the hardware store with it, and when the old ladies who ran the Connot Dress Shoppe and Lu Ann's Women's Clothes and Cadwell Shoes retired or died, the vacant storefronts were soon filled with gift shops and galleries showcasing west-

ern art and handcrafted jewelry. A computer store replaced
a barbershop. A metaphysical bookstore popped up on
First Street, candles and totems and tarot decks displayed
alongside exotic dresses made by the indigenous people of
impoverished exotic countries.

THE BODY ART WORKSHOP was open until nine o'clock at
night. I usually spent my evenings there, talking with Slade
and watching him work. Eventually the scumble of flash
designs separated into individual images. Some of the designs were artistic; others were amateurish and loppy. Slade
hung new sheets on the wall every few weeks, but he kept
tattooing the same designs over and over. The twenty-five-
dollar rose. The thirty-five-dollar rose. Cartoon characters
and one particular panther that Slade brought practically to
life with the judicious use of frost-blue highlighting along
edges of solid black.

One evening, I arrived at the shop just as three college
boys were leaving. I looked at the stencils on the counter.
"Two Yosemite Sams?" I asked. "Why would they get that
when they could have anything at all?"

Slade shrugged. "Some people are like that. They want
tattoos so bad that the desire is bigger than anything about
the design, and somewhere way back in the corners of their
minds, most people think that their choices are limited to
the tattoos they've seen on other people, but that's not
what they're thinking when they get tattooed. I bet that
those three kids think they've just gotten the most original
tattoos in the whole world."

Despite the occasional misguided Tasmanian Devils and Yosemite Sams, tattooing seemed honest. I believed that tattooed people had chosen to display the most genuine aspects of their souls upon their skin. I wished that I were brave enough to be so truthful, wished that I had something important enough to communicate that tattooing would be the only way to say it.

In two years, I had spent so much time with Slade and his customers that tattooing had begun to unfurl into a language all its own, and reading it was like deciphering the hieroglyphic variables of a vaguely complex equation. I am x plus I love y and I've been *pi times the radius squared*, but I wish I were n. Ten minutes of casual conversation with a tattooed person was all it took to fine-tune the distinctions between *I am* and *I wish*. It was metaphor in its purest form. It was poetry.

Chapter Three

THE MAN SPRAWLED in the tattoo chair looked as though he hadn't slept well. He was tall and lanky, with the build so common among men who work with cars—skinny legs, a tiny ass, and a bouquet of tendon and muscle erupting from a taut waist. His shoulders were broad, his arms well-muscled and sleeved with tattoos. His face was all angular planes and carved cheekbones, with a right-angle set to the hinges of his jaw. His eyes were brown like wildwood and gleaming between cranberry creases. One of his pant legs was pulled up to the knee and Slade was bent over his leg, tattooing intently. The buzzing sound of the tattoo machine mixed with the bass beat of the Suicidal Tendencies tape, and Slade sang along.

"What are you getting?" I asked.

"Mr. No Credit," Slade laughed.

I leaned forward and examined the tattoo, a bust of a skull in a fedora hat and a pinstripe suit, with the words "Mr. No Credit" arced above the hat in a fancy script. Slade was watching as though he expected me to laugh at a joke he'd just told, and was disappointed that the punch line had eluded me.

"Rick deals," Slade explained, wiping down the reddened outline. "He's Mr. No Credit."

"Hey, man," Rick waved a hand in my direction.

"Aw, Karol's cool." Slade changed machines and lined up the shader needles in a flat tube. He adjusted the rheostat and began to color in the tattoo. "Rick's in a cash-only business. No credit. Get it?"

Rick sat through the tattoo as though it was nothing, as though it didn't hurt a bit. He talked about cars, about his straight job in a body shop, and his stories were filled with talk of pistons and gears, connecting rods and fluid couplings. He had generous lips that framed straight white teeth beneath a downy mustache. I was mesmerized by his soft, husky voice, and the changing shape of his mouth as he spoke. The more I looked, the more attractive he seemed. Every time he caught my eye, he graced me with a beaming smile and a salacious wink. I knew he couldn't be any older than I was, but something more aged than his years peeked through a surface air of guile and innocence, a hint of the old man he might someday become. Something else peeked through, too, something dangerous and intriguing.

When Mr. No Credit was done, Rick stood up and ran his hands through his unkempt hair. "Man, that hurt like a motherfucker, right there on the shinbone."

"Looks cool, though," Slade said. He locked up the shop and the three of us went to the Buckhorn Bar for a beer. We sat at a table with deep initials carved into the wood and ordered Budweiser long-necks. Slade lit a cigarette, which wasn't enough to disguise nearly a century of stale smoke and the scent of spilled alcohol percolating beneath the linoleum.

"When I first opened the shop," Slade said, "some guy in Denver sent a few henchmen up to shut me down. They rolled up outside the shop—"

"Henchmen?" I asked.

"Yeah. So anyway, they rolled up outside the shop, pushed the door open, and—"

"Where do you get henchmen?" I asked.

"I've got henchmen," Rick said.

"Can I have a couple?" I asked politely.

"You can't *have* them," he said. "It's more of a rent-to-own kind of thing."

Slade leaned forward to recapture our attention. "So these big dudes roll up—"

"What exactly do henchmen do?" I asked Rick.

"Anything you want." He smiled. "Depends on the price."

"I'd like a couple of henchmen." I leaned toward Rick, flirting with my body and my smile.

"I'll see what I can do." He was flirting right back, his head cocked to one side, eyes flashing, and his mouth turned up in a crooked smile.

"Yeah, these big dudes rolled up and told me that they weren't going to mess me up in my shop in broad daylight, but that if they ever saw me on the street, I was a dead man." Slade spoke quickly and sat back, waiting for a response.

"If you have henchmen," I asked Rick, "can you dress them any way you want?"

"Probably. For a price." Rick drained his beer. "Sometimes, though, they have their own outfits, something that makes them feel especially henchy. Like big boots and one of those wallets on a chain."

"What do you want henchmen for?" Slade looked concerned.

"Nothing really." I shrugged and smiled. "I'd just like to be able to walk in somewhere and say, 'Hi, I'm Karol, and these are my henchmen.'"

"You ought to take 'em to that yuppie vegetarian place," Rick laughed. He mimicked my voice, pitching it high and mean: "'I'll have a plate of sprouts and bring some tofu for my henchmen.'"

RICK SPENT AN increasing amount of time with Slade and, consequently, with me. He spent a lot of time and money in the tattoo shop, and after he'd acquired a set of facing, screaming skulls on his rib cage, skulls bigger than Rick's own head, I was overcome with the desire to photograph him. Rick was reluctant.

"I like your pictures, don't get me wrong," Rick said. "But some people just don't look good flat."

I pleaded. I cajoled. I flirted. An hour later, we were in the Rainbow Photography studio. Rick took off his shirt and folded his tattooed arms across his tattooed chest, watching intently as I set up the lights and tripod. He didn't speak at all, but he let me pose him however I wanted. When I was done, he put his shirt back on and helped me put away the lights. He cradled my camera in his hands before setting it gently in the bag.

"What do you want to do now?" he asked.

"I'm going to go home and develop this film," I said.

"Want some company?"

My darkroom was a poorly ventilated closet above the stairs that led to my apartment. Rick followed me in and stood behind me as I aligned the film in a negative carrier and put it into the enlarger. He leaned forward and watched intently as the timer clicked away the exposure, a negative image of Rick's face and shoulders on a piece of shiny paper curling slightly on the base of the enlarger. While we waited, Rick told me stories of the cars he had known, and I strained to hear the soft, husky sounds of his voice over the clicking timer. I was conscious of the smell of him behind me. Brut and gasoline, shampoo and grease and sweet breath.

I touched his paper face in the developer tray, caressing his cheekbones with my fingertips in the chemical bath. The warmth brings out the details; the heat of a single finger can bring shadows to a place that looks empty. I lifted the print with tongs and moved it from the developer to the stop bath, from the stop to the fix tray.

"What's that?" Rick reached past me to dip a finger in a chemical tray. "Tastes like salad dressing," he said, sucking his finger thoughtfully.

"Fix," I said. "It stops the action of the developer and makes the paper insensitive to light."

"I could use some of that." Rick laughed. "Yeah, fix me up good."

Rick stayed in the darkroom with me while I printed every negative. I washed the prints in my bathtub, and arranged the wet photographs in a half circle on the living-room floor. Rick leaned forward from the edge of the couch as though he were mustering the nerve to look at the pictures up close.

His eyes ran back and forth over the photographs of himself, and I couldn't tell if he liked them or not, and I was trying to find the words to ask him when he leaned over and kissed me, his tongue exploring the corners of my surprised lips.

"I'm sorry." Rick picked up a handful of not-yet-dry photographs of himself and hurried to the door. He wouldn't meet my eyes. He ran down the stairs and peeled out.

The next day, Slade gave me a weird, fishy look when I walked by the tattoo shop after work. I waved, but didn't stop. He came out onto the sidewalk. "What's wrong with you?" he asked impatiently.

I stammered as I told Slade about Rick.

"You want me to have a talk with him? I'll tell him not to overstep his bounds."

"No. That's okay. I'm not mad at him. I—" I stopped, staring at the ground and searching for the right words.

"What?" Slade tipped my chin up with a gloved hand. "You can't be serious. What do you want with Rick? The boy couldn't outwit stucco." Slade snorted and shook his head. "I'm sure he's yours for the taking." He turned around and slammed into the tattoo shop, and I didn't blame him for being angry. Slade and I had rules about dating each other's friends. Well, one rule, really, which was that we didn't. Even so, I wanted Rick.

That night, I went to Rick's house to finish what he'd started. As soon as he opened the door, I kissed him hard and jumped onto his bed, hoping to strike an alluring pose. A ratchet handle dug uncomfortably into my thigh, and I spent several minutes tossing clothing and tools off the bed while Rick stood, perplexed, in the doorway. I smiled and held out my arms, sitting on the bed like the princess of Snap-On tools and greasy coveralls.

Rick's hands were hesitant at first, as though he couldn't decide whether he ought to take off my clothing or his own. He wriggled a hand under my skirt and up my thigh, and his fingers slipped under the waistband of my underwear. I could see his heart beating in his chest, beneath a tattooed demon. I reached up, cupped his face in my hands, and pulled his mouth to mine.

He ran his hands up my sides, callused thumbs thrumming across my ribs and breasts. Up the undersides of my arms, tickling and pushing them over my head. He leaned forward and his hair brushed my cheeks, and the tattoos on his arms rippled and flexed as he moved.

He was everything I thought I wanted, wild and sensuous. Funny, too, and a little bit dangerous, with his crooked smile and deep eyes like a calm, dark sea with a dangerous undertow. A woman could lose herself in eyes like those.

IF YOUR BEST FRIEND is a tattoo artist, there's no stigma, no negative stereotype associated with tattooing. It's art and a little bit of pain. No mystery. Tattooing is a simple process, really, and its simplicity belies its permanence. A tattoo is created by embedding pigment in skin. Tattoo needles are solid, not hollow; they don't inject anything. Ink slides down the needles as they penetrate the epidermis, and the skin treats a tattoo like any other wound, knitting itself back together over the tiny pigment puddles that adhere to cells in the underlying elastic pad of tissue. When it's healed, the tattoo is visible through a thin layer of scar tissue that feels just like the rest. Tattooed skin is just as ticklish, just as warm.

"YOU READY?" Slade tugged on a pair of latex gloves.

I nodded. I was facedown on the dentist's chair in the

back room of the tattoo shop. My knees were bent backwards and locked into place, sticking out stiffly from the
curve on the lower end of the chair. My face was stuck between the prongs of the headrest, its metal rods pressing
against my cheeks while my forehead fused to the vinyl.

Slade started at the bottom, right below my ribs. The
first few minutes of the outline weren't too bad. After a
half hour or so, the scratching of the needles and the sound
of the machine and the pressure of Slade's elbow in the
small of my back were making me crazy. The sounds of the
tattoo machine were intensified, wet and sloppy buzzing in
the ink cup, insects in the air above my back, muffled chop-
ping sounds as they punctured the skin. At first, the cool
spray of the green soap was a welcome respite from the
needles, but the repeated wiping became agonizing. I
cringed every time I heard Slade refolding a paper towel, an-
ticipating the burning tug of the towel pulling at the abra-
sion of my fresh tattoo with the pressure of Slade's knuckles
behind it.

My spine was curved the wrong way, my vertebrae
were cracking under the pressure of a facedown position
in a chair designed for face-up comfort, and my feet fell
asleep. I switched my focus back and forth between the
metal rods supporting the headrest and the linoleum tiles
on the floor. I counted the spangles in one of the square
tiles — eighty-seven — and multiplied the spangles by all the
tiles I could see without turning my neck. Then I counted
the specks between the spangles and multiplied them.

I'd heard Slade's customers talking about what their

tattoos meant, why they'd chosen a particular design. I'd learned to read the meanings behind the images so easily that tattooing had become a beautiful sort of visual verse. And here I was, getting a tattoo that marked neither milestone nor accomplishment, a tattoo that revealed nothing about my personality. It wouldn't say anything about anyplace I'd been (except, obviously, the tattoo shop) or anything I'd done. My half-outlined tattoo was destined to be mute.

"Do you think I should have gotten something more personal?" I asked.

Slade laughed. "This is going to be part of your person for the rest of your life."

"I mean, something more...I don't know...significant?"

"How many tattoos do I have?" Slade asked.

"I don't know."

"Me either. How many of them do you think I got because I needed to remind myself of one specific thing? All of them? I'm not 'Slade the Human Bulletin Board.' I've got exactly one that means anything more than tattoo art, and it's small. I would have gotten something completely different if I'd just wanted another tattoo."

"Which one?" I asked.

"It's a secret," Slade said. "Why do you think it's a picture instead of words?"

"But other people talk about what their tattoos mean. Sometimes you can tell just by looking at them."

"It doesn't mean half as much to most of them as you

think. Sometimes they just need an excuse, or maybe they wish it meant something and maybe it will someday."

I concentrated on my breathing, ragged and raspy. In and out. Slade rested one hand lightly on my skin while he dipped the needles in the ink, an illusion of comfort. His palm pushed against my skin as he stretched it, pulling it away from my spine. His hand seemed heavier and heavier, pushing the air out of my lungs until each breath became a conscious effort. The needles tickled along my ribs and didn't hurt much on the flat part of my shoulder blade, but they caused a headache-inducing pain on my spine and rattled my teeth as they flew along the back edges of my collarbone. I willed my muscles to relax, begged my mind to ignore the pain, which had become routine, boring, in its sameness.

I closed my eyes and thought about the drawing taped to the wall above the ink rack. Slade glanced at it occasionally to make sure that the tattooed lines matched the penciled ones. I listened to my heartbeat and imagined my blood rushing white cells to the area of invasion, fighting against what my mind had decided to do. Beneath the beautiful design that was slowly becoming part of my skin, my blood was busy carting the excess ink off to the nearest lymph node for storage.

I tried to distract myself by thinking up interesting little fictions strung together with gossamer strands of half-truths, stories I could tell later when someone asked me why I'd gotten tattooed. I imagined the words I'd use to describe this image as a profound articulation of my inner being, and even though my side of this imaginary conversation was mostly lies, I wondered why I'd even bother telling anyone something so intimate. I was embarrassed for myself in the same way I was embarrassed for the people who bared intimate and tawdry details about their personal lives on TV talk shows.

If anyone asked, I'd make up something really fabulous, something straight from a turn-of-the-century circus sideshow. It would be a story that changed from time to time, from town to town, of course, like those of the sideshow tattooed ladies in the 1930s. They were stoic and proud and serious as could be, telling audience after audience about the tribe of "savages" who'd abducted them. They didn't really get the savages' names, even though they'd been held captive long enough to be tattooed from head to toe with traditional American designs.

Slade unclipped the power cord from his machine and wiped my back one last time. He helped me up, held out a hand mirror, and positioned me in front of the big mirror on the wall.

I have become a work of art. That was my first thought, my only thought, really. The outline of an Oriental dragon stretched from my collarbone to my waist, writhing along my ribs and across my spine. I looked over my shoulder at the big picture. A riot of Manic Panic Plum purple hair and dark red lipstick. The diamond that Rick gave me sparkling on the side of my nose. Japanese-animation eyes rimmed with kohl.

"In the old days," Slade said, "people thought dragon tattoos were charms for safety. They got them for protection."

"Protection from what?"

Slade shrugged. "Whatever they were afraid of, I guess."

THE PINNACLE OF my photography career was a solo exhibition at the Melville C. Brown Gallery, a block north of the tattoo shop, in 1989. A week before the opening reception, I carried four years' worth of black-and-white photographs of heavily tattooed people, into the empty gallery space. After I left, the gallery owner arranged them on the walls as she saw fit.

The photographs had been framed one at a time, whenever I could afford it. I'd never hung them all on my walls, had never seen them all at once. One at a time, they were exactly what I'd wanted. I assumed the individuality of each person in each photograph would be amplified when they were all together, but it didn't work like that at all. Some sort of artistic circumlocution had taken place, and the tattoos in the photographs were right back where they'd started, images on paper. It was as though the camera had pulled back from the close-up of the image each tattoo had come from and—surprise!—the pictures weren't flat or on paper, couldn't be thrown away or erased. I would have been embarrassed if I hadn't been quite so amused by the irony of it all. I'd put the tattoo images right back where they'd started—on a wall. If Lewis

Carroll had written a tattoo shop into Wonderland, this would have been it.

"*Y*OU MAKE YOUR choices and you live with them." There was no sympathy in Slade's voice. The gallery show was over, and the backseat of my car was loaded with framed photographs. I was still feeling sorry for myself. It was maybe two o'clock in the morning, and we were in my car, between parties. Slade reached under his shirt and pulled a shiny Glock pistol out of the waistband of his pants. *Interesting,* I thought. *You never can tell what people have under their clothes.* Slade pressed the button on his armrest that lowered the electric window, stuck the gun out, and began firing up into the air. I reached down to the buttons on my armrest, which controlled every window in the car, rolled up Slade's window with his arm in it, pressed the lock button, and continued driving at a reasonable speed. Having the window most of the way up muffled the sounds of the gunshots and made it a little easier to concentrate on my driving.

When the clip was empty, I rolled down the window and Slade pulled his arm and the gun into the car.

"How do you feel about President Bush?" he asked.

"I didn't vote for him."

"I did." Slade shoved the Glock back into his pants.

"Why?"

"Love the guy. Look what he's done for tattooing. We've got a whole generation of yuppies who can't wait to get tattooed. They're bored, they're greedy, they can remember when the salad days meant drugs and sex and rock and roll."

Slade reached into his pocket and pulled out a small bag of pot and a package of rolling papers. He rolled a one-handed fat joint, licked the edge of the paper, and twirled the ends shut.

"You're still having your salad days," I pointed out.

"Yeah, but a lot of people aren't. They've wussed out. Getting a tattoo is the most daring thing they'll ever do. There's no spiritual meaning to it anymore. It's not even a rebellion—tattoos are material goods in a material culture, and that cheesy Yosemite Sam or whatever is the one thing you can take with you when your wussed-out yuppie life is over."

Slade lit the joint, sucked in a big hit, and passed it my way. "You're a pretty good artist," he said, without exhaling. "I've been thinking it's time for an apprentice in the shop. Gotta carry on the tradition." He pointed at me and winked.

"Me? Are you serious?"

"As a heart attack." Slade grinned. "You can start tomorrow."

I dropped him off and drove home. A police car was waiting outside my house. I hesitated for a moment, thought about driving around the block and sneaking down the alley on foot. Even though I wasn't the one shooting a gun out of a car window, I wasn't sure how they might feel about the kind of person who would just roll up the window and drive on while the obviously bad person, the one with the gun, kept shooting. It was late, though, and I was too tired to try to hide. I pretended that the police weren't there, weren't waiting and watching. I willed myself invisible and parked the car.

"Over here." A policeman finger wagged at me through the window of the cop car. I walked to the middle of the street, leaned over, and looked into the car. Everything metal gleamed in the streetlight—badges, bullets, flashlight handles—but it was too dark to see their faces.

"Did you get him home all right?"

I nodded.

"Be careful." The window whizzed up, and the police car pulled away from the curb.

"You make your choices and you live with them," I said to the taillights. I carried my photographs inside and shoved them into the back of a closet.

I was on my way to becoming a tattoo artist.

Chapter Four

A GRAPEFRUIT SLATHERED in petroleum jelly is quite possibly the most slippery object in the world, especially if you're trying to hold the grapefruit in one hand while tattooing it with the other.

You can't start right in tattooing on human skin—I mean, you *can,* and some people *do,* but when you think about it, this isn't a very good idea. So many elements to consider, like depth and angle and grain and control. There's more to tattooing than needles and skin; you have to consider the responsibility inherent in the business of transforming other people's bodies, other people's lives. It's best to start with a grapefruit and practice under the tutelage of someone who knows what he's doing.

At first, my tattoo apprenticeship seemed more like indentured servitude, but I didn't mind. I was filled with self-importance as I unlocked the door of the shop. I trotted around behind Slade like a gleeful puppy, tidying up the shop between appointments and watching him work. I scoured stainless-steel needle tubes with a toothbrush and pipe cleaners before sterilizing them in the autoclave. I made stencils and ran Slade's errands. I mixed finely powdered concentrated colors with vodka, distilled water, and a splash of glycerine, secretly proud of the rainbow stains left by the inevitable dusty pigment cloud, the colors vivid and semipermanent on my hands, my arms, my face.

I apprenticed in the tattoo shop six days a week. On Mondays, when the shop was closed, I worked in a bookstore around the corner. I managed to scrape by on food stamps and the cash I earned by holding the hands of frightened (or more often, lecherous) tattoo clients for five dollars each.

During the first three weeks of my apprenticeship, I never touched a tattoo machine. I was beginning to think I'd never get a chance to actually tattoo, that apprenticing was nothing more than an exercise in janitorial work. This made me grumpy, but I didn't know what to say. I just kept picking up dirty paper towels and vacuuming, with increasing resentment.

One day, I slammed open the door of the tattoo shop, determined to speak my mind. Slade was one step ahead of me.

"Don't say it," he said, smiling. "I know. You're sick of the bullshit, right? You want to tattoo, right? You wonder why I've made you do all the grunt work around here."

His words paralyzed my icy pre-argument frown.

"Humility, doll." He laughed. "It's not all about ink and skin. You've got to learn to have the right attitude — otherwise, you'll go down in flames. But I've got a surprise for you. Today, you tattoo." Slade handed me a pair of latex gloves and set a cup of black ink and a cup of petroleum jelly in the ink rack. He took out his liner, showed me how to assemble the needlebar and the tube and attach it to the machine. He pressed the foot pedal, and the machine hummed merrily in his hand. Slade reached under the counter and pulled out a grapefruit. He demonstrated proper depth, speed, and angle, deftly freehanding a gruesome skull on the grapefruit. He treated the grapefruit like a customer, like it was a real tattoo on a real person. He rubbed the grapefruit skin with petroleum jelly as he worked, and wiped away the excess ink with a paper towel wound between the fingers of his working hand.

Slade tossed a second grapefruit at me, handed over the machine. "If you go too deep," he said, "it'll squirt you in the eye."

I tried to do what he had done, but the machine, which had seemed weightless when it was resting in my palm, became unwieldy and painfully heavy when I tried to hold it properly, gripping the tube like a pencil and balancing the weight of the machine in the air above my thumb. I rubbed a glob of petroleum jelly on the surface of the grapefruit, dipped the needles into the cup of black ink, and pressed the foot pedal. The machine shook with power, fast vibrations that rattled my hand.

As soon as the needles touched it, the grapefruit popped out of my hand and rolled onto the floor. I retrieved it, then managed to skewer it on the needles, causing a great burst of grapefruit juice to shoot into my eye. By the time Slade returned, I was covered with black ink and Vaseline. My hair was decorated with sticky juice and pulp, and I was sobbing quietly. The sting of grapefruit juice in my eye was only part of it. Slade had made tattooing look virtually effortless, and I was disappointed to find that it was not.

"Lighten up," Slade said. "You'll get the hang of it. We've got plenty of grapefruit and all day to practice." He sat next to me while I tried again, laughed when the grapefruit jumped out of my hands.

"Can't I take the gloves off?" I asked. "It might be easier. I'm almost certain that I could hold on to it if I didn't have to wear the gloves."

"Nope. Here's a tip, though. Don't cover the whole thing with Vaseline. It's not a sex toy that you're trying to lubricate; you just want the ink to pool up in a line, so you can see where you're going. Just put a little dab on the part you're working. Wipe it off when you're ready to move on."

I set my jaw and tried again. I made a wiggly line. I was tattooing.

My hand ached from the strain of the tattoo machine when I woke up the next morning. I couldn't quite get all the dried pulp and black ink washed out of my hair, and I was hoping this day would be better. Easier. Maybe the shop would be really busy, and there wouldn't be time for my lesson. Maybe I'd have to spend the whole day tidying up after Slade.

Four grapefruits were sitting in a row in the curve on the dentist's chair in Slade's tattoo room. Three of them were plain, just hunkering there, but the fourth had been stenciled with a panther head from one of the flash sheets that hung in the front room. Its hollow purple eyes gazed at me malevolently.

Slade pointed at each grapefruit in turn. "Circles," he said. "Squares. The alphabet. Then do that one." He smiled and pointed at the panther grapefruit.

I fitted a needlebar into a tube and clamped it into the machine. I pulled on a pair of gloves and sat down to my work. I made circles, which was much harder than I had expected. I tattooed big circles and little circles, lopsided, wonky circles, none of them completely closed. The needles skittled across the grain of the grapefruit skin as though my machine had a mind of its own.

Squares were just as bad. I couldn't draw a straight line on a round, pocky surface, and the lines refused to meet at the corners, but I didn't get half as much grapefruit juice in my eyes as I had the day before. It was late afternoon before I was ready to try the panther. I ignored the screaming muscles in my hand and gritted my teeth. After I outlined the panther head, I washed off the grapefruit and held it up. Slade examined it closely, praising some lines and criticizing others. I took it home like a proud parent, cradling it in my lap and staring lovingly at it as I drove. I put it on the coffee table and admired it all evening.

The next day, a banana was lying on the chair like a minimalist still life. I was relieved when Slade reached for the banana, peeled it, and popped it into his mouth. He pulled another banana out from under the counter and handed it to me.

"No, oo cand eab dabt." Slade shook his head frantically as he swallowed. "Don't eat it." He fitted a shader bar, seven needles stacked four-on-three and offset at a fraction of an angle, into a flat tube and affixed it to my machine. "Color it in," he said.

"Color what in?"

"The whole thing. Solid."

It took me all day to make a not-quite-ripe banana solid black. I held up the mushy result for Slade's approval, a hopeful smile coloring my face.

"Man, if that were a person, he'd be in a heap of hurt," Slade said. "See this? Hamburger. It's going to scab up bad. The ink's going to fall out with the scabs, and leave one mean-looking scar. That's not a tattoo, that's maiming."

"I'm sorry," I said, more to the banana than to Slade.

"Well, you've got to know when you're doing it wrong so you'll know when you're doing it right." Slade picked up a new banana and the shader machine. He showed me how to use the shader properly, pushing the needles against the grain of the banana peel in small circles, back and forth, never digging too deeply into the peel. When he was done, his banana still looked like a banana, only black.

I practiced for weeks, practiced until my apartment was littered with tattooed fruit in various stages of decay, practiced until Slade said, "You've got to find yourself a guinea pig. You know, someone who will let you tattoo them, even though they know it's your first time."

"Rick," I said. The only thing Rick liked better than tattoos was fast cars.

Slade nodded and laughed. "There you go."

On the off-chance that Rick might balk at this opportunity, I drew up a special piece before I asked him. A swirly, art nouveau, tribal piece that, from the right angle, spelled out Cuda, Rick's all-time favorite car. The way I figured it, I could draw "Cuda" in big block letters, offer to tattoo it on Rick's forehead, and he wouldn't even hesitate.

Rick was lying on a creeper underneath a car when I pulled into his driveway.

"Hey," I said, "do you want another tattoo? For free?"

"What?" The heels of his boots churned up a small dust storm as he kicked the creeper out from under his car. I knelt down beside the rear fender and held out the drawing. Rick frowned and ran a grease-covered hand through his wild hair. I turned the design sideways, and he sucked in his breath.

"'Cuda'?"

I nodded and smiled.

"Right on. When can we do it?"

The next night, after the paying customers left, Slade locked up the tattoo shop and turned the OPEN sign around to the side that said WILL RETURN AT above a plastic clock face with adjustable red plastic hands. Rick sat down in the chair and tugged the leg of his pants up to his knee. I shaved his calf with a straight-edge razor held with shaky fingers. I did everything just the way Slade had taught me, rubbing musk-scented Mennen Speed Stick deodorant across a folded paper towel and wiping it across Rick's skin. I put the drawing on a sheet of ditto master, ran it through the thermofax, and pressed it against Rick's skin. Slade sat in a chair with his arms folded, watching me.

"You realize," Slade said, "that tattooing is an enormous responsibility. You are changing another person, and I don't mean just by the ink in their skin. You have the power to create something that can change a person's life forever, and this is both good and bad."

I rolled my eyes. If anyone should know how tattooing changes your outlook on life, it was the three of us. I was three months into my apprenticeship, fifty hours into tattoos of my own, and going on two years as Slade's best friend.

"This is more than a job." Slade leaned forward and stared into my eyes. "You can't take it lightly. Even though tattoos are material goods in a consumer culture, a tattoo is also a primal scream, permanently etched into the skin." Slade leaned back and lit a cigarette.

"Wow, man," Rick said. "That's intense. I never thought about it like that."

"I come up with some pretty deep shit when I'm stoned," Slade said.

It was just like Slade to say something profound and chalk it up to marijuana. He didn't seem to want anyone to know that he was a thinker, that he lay awake at night, stone-cold sober, pondering his life and the responsibilities it entailed. I'd seen him do it. Of course, I'd also seen the other nights, when it all got to be too much, and Slade fired up his bong, time and time again until he nodded off to sleep, accompanied by the television turned up so loud that it drowned out the possibility of words or thought.

I assembled my machine and pulled on a pair of gloves. I stared hard at the stencil because my only other choice was to look Rick in the eye and give him an opportunity to change his mind.

"Go ahead and start," Slade said. "That stencil's ready and we don't have all night."

"I don't think it's quite dry," I said. I smudged a finger across the purple outline, and the stencil smeared away from the line. "See? I think we'd better wait just a little bit longer." I knew how to tattoo, in theory. That wasn't the problem. I didn't want to hurt Rick, which was sort of silly when I thought about it. He knew how it was going to feel. He wanted me to do it. So hurting Rick wasn't really the problem either. I wondered how much of Slade's speech was metaphorical, wondered whether I really would be tying myself to tattooing for the rest of my life the moment I touched the needles to Rick's skin.

I looked at the machine in my hand, the dry stencil on Rick's leg. It wasn't too late to back out.

Then the thrill set in, a combination of fear and uncertainty and adrenaline mingled with glee and uncontrollable excitement. The thrill coursed through me like electricity, and the pulse of my own blood pounded in my throat. I looked down at the tattoo machine I was holding, and my hand felt like it belonged to someone else, cold and distant. I tucked a folded paper towel under the machine and between the first two fingers, wound it around the hand, tucked it under the fingers and pressed them hard against the palm, and pretended that Rick's leg was just a great big banana. I dabbed a bit of petroleum jelly on the edge of the stencil, dipped the needles into a cup of ink, pressed the foot pedal, and traced the needles along the stencil line on Rick's skin.

The result was a black smear punctuated with dots of overspray, which wasn't altogether unlike the excess ink that pooled up along any line Slade tattooed. I twisted my hand to squeegee and mop with the ever-ready paper towel, just like Slade always did. Any similarity between Slade tattooing and what I'd done ended there; beneath the excess ink was nothing more than a pinkish line and a couple of black squiggles. This wasn't like tattooing a banana. It wasn't anything like that at all.

"You can't be afraid of hurting him," Slade said. "Just concentrate and do your job."

I squinted until everything about Rick was outside my

field of vision, before going over the same inch-long line, slower and deeper. The line was solid this time, so I kept going without waiting for Slade's reaction. Before long, I was lost in the sensation, and the vibrations from the machine sang along the nerves of my hand and flickered up the insides of my wrists.

Layer after layer, latex like the connecting wall of a dividing cell. On either side, skin—his and mine—and beneath that, muscle and bone, nerve endings and blood. The heat that rose from Rick's body was markedly more pronounced on the freshly tattooed part, cooler outside the lines.

After the outline was done, I changed to a shading machine and nine-needle magnum. I was ink-blind within an hour; Rick's tattoo turned itself upside down and backwards and floated over each of my eyes like a levitating cataract or a pirate's eye-patch waiting to be squared up. I stared myself into a half-hypnotic state in which the differences between animate and inanimate were both exaggerated and overlapping. Like an LSD trip, everything blended together, yet was distinctly separate. Rick's breathing was a measured, exacting rhythm. I found myself holding my breath from time to time—forgetting, actually, to let the air in and out—and trying to catch up with hungry, ragged whooshes. It seemed there was no stopping, that I was compelled to color Rick's body cell by cell, no matter how long it took, a tattoo purgatory from which there was no escape, but which was actually quite nice once you got used to it.

Several hours later, the Cuda tattoo was solid black with a halo of red inflammation. The pores were enlarged, like the pocks on an orange peel, exactly the way Slade said skin would look when it had been worked enough. I spritzed Rick's leg with liquid green soap, coated the tattoo lightly with petroleum jelly to keep the blood from welling up, and sat back while Slade and Rick examined my work. Slade arched his eyebrows like he was pleasantly surprised, and gave me a little nod. I grinned, biting my lower lip to keep from laughing with satisfaction and pride.

Rick ran one finger tentatively along the redness next to the tattoo. "Didn't hurt a bit," he said.

I looked at Rick's welted, orange-peel skin colored solid black. Blood oozed through the ink, and when I looked up, Rick's face was white except for two splotchy circles on his cheeks. I was grateful for his lie.

Chapter Five

IMAGINE THAT YOU'RE new in town, and you just love Laramie. People are walking the streets wearing cowboy hats, and there are real guns tacked to rear windows in more than a few pickup trucks. People are so nice here, they really are, always stopping to help you fix a flat tire or offer directions when you lose your way. Say you've just moved into a nice little ranchette, a Victorian-style house on ten treeless acres of prairie not five minutes north of town. The house is brand-new, built on spec to appeal to someone with your cosmopolitan tastes. You've planted a few saplings, tied them to delineator posts, and shrouded them with burlap so that the wind won't send them flying onto the neighboring ranchette.

Maybe the first thing you'll notice is how big the West is, how the prairie and the sky go on forever, how the thin air at 7,200 feet makes everything look a little bit farther away. You are awed by the limitless textures and the vast expanse of the place you now call home. Maybe you realize that your concept of western space had been shaped by television boundaries.

The land beneath your new home was part of a working ranch not that long ago, and you have found any number of bleached cattle bones on your property. You take them for your carcass art collection. The walkway from your red-dirt lane to your front door is limned with a delightful arrangement of skulls and femurs, tilted pelvic bones and rakish lower jaws. These bones have everything to do with aesthetics and nothing to do with death. You paint a dreamcatcher on the forehead of a steer skull. Although this skull, like the others, belonged to an animal that most likely froze to death if it wasn't eaten alive by coyotes or mistaken for a bull elk during hunting season, you nail it to the post beneath your mailbox without thinking about the skull's past; as far as you're concerned, bones aren't meaningful until you've boiled them for an afternoon to get rid of germs and other icky souvenirs of life. You bleach, you paint, you polish.

You'll need a pickup truck, of course, four-wheel-drive, or maybe a sports utility vehicle for the western excursions you plan to take. Even if you don't drive that far off asphalt, you've heard about the snow, about the drifts and the wind; a reliable western vehicle is going to be absolutely necessary if you're going to make it to town for groceries and whatnot in the winter.

Maybe you'll wear boots and Levi's every day, whether or not you have horses, just because you can, just because you live in the West now. The radio in your truck is forever set on a Top 40 country station.

Say it's a Saturday night and you're headed for the Cowboy Saloon. You pull up next to a red-mud-splattered truck that has a picture of a brand and the name of a ranch on the driver's door. Three men are in the cab, their cowboy hats squeezed together so tightly that it seems the hats must have gone in first, that the bodies must have followed in a slow and synchronized ritual.

These are real cowboys, in the sense that they are men who work with livestock and barbed wire year-round. The boots are the first telltale sign. Shined up or not doesn't matter; it's whether or not they fit and how many blisters piled up getting them that way. It's whether the boots cause a man to walk with self-conscious bravado or unconscious grace. A boot's heel is meant for stirrup stability, and if a man doesn't know his boots on the ground, he'll pitch forward like a woman in unfamiliar pumps or limp on his blisters like a greenhorn. The hats are another dead giveaway, because function and form fuse at the hairline, and a hat becomes personal. When a man spends that much time with his head tucked into something that shields him from sun and snow while shaping itself to his skull, a Saturday-night hat just doesn't feel right. It doesn't fit the same, and it smells like Resistol instead of hardworking sweat.

As the cowboys get out of the truck, maybe you'll notice that they're wearing Wrangler jeans, not Levi's, like you've got on. Ranchers and cowboys wear Wranglers because they fit tight in the ass and thighs, don't work their way painfully up the crotch, one wrinkle at a time, while a person's on horseback, the way Levi's do. Levi's were miner's pants. They were designed for men who made a living in cramped dark spaces underground, bending over and sorting rocks. Levi's were cut for squatting, constructed from stiff denim meant to shield the lower half of a person from rock-scraped knees, collapsing tunnels, or the dangerous combination of a miner's wandering thoughts and a temperamental pickax. Wranglers, on the other hand, were designed for legs shaped by a stirrup-to-stirrup arc, cut for motion, and named after the ranch hands who wore them instead of the man who thought them up.

Maybe you expect the cowboys to be taciturn and introspective, because that's how it is in the movies. Maybe you follow them into the Cowboy Saloon with all the eager anticipation of a theater patron. Maybe it comes as a great surprise when one of them lights a menthol cigarette, huffing and puffing and lighting the next one off the butt of the first. Maybe your thoughts about legislative restrictions on smoking—which can kill you, even secondhand—are interrupted by a loud wolf whistle or a lewd comment, something along the lines of "check out the rack on that one," which causes all three cowboy hats to bob with every jiggle and sway of a college girl easing her way toward the dance floor. The cowboy closest to you taps a can of Copenhagen against his palm while he describes in graphic detail what he could do with a college girl like that, how he'd like to rope and brand her (this with a pelvic thrust that has nothing, you hope, to do with identifying livestock).

Maybe, while he opens the tin of chewing tobacco and orders another round of tequila shooters, his companions laugh and tell him that the college girl ain't the type to have anything to do with him, that he's no better than a rodeo cowboy, thinking eight seconds is a good ride. As he packs his molars with a wad of chew that transcends "just a pinch between cheek and gum," he muses aloud about whether or not the college girl has a thing for cowboys, rodeo or real. He'll decide she must, being as how she's in a cowboy bar, never mind the fakers.

Maybe he looks at you when he says this.

As you're trying to reconcile the West of your imagination with what you've just witnessed, the cowboy moseys onto the dance floor and emerges from the crowd with his arm draped loosely around the shoulders of the college girl and a six-pack of Budweiser in his hand. This is worse than you thought. It's drunken, debauched. Where is the cowboy who was supposed to come with those clothes and that truck, the man with the squinty-eyed affinity for cattle and schoolmarms? Where is your western hero?

THAT STORY PASSED through the tattoo shop in versions and fragments and variations on a theme, usually delivered

by someone who was getting a first tattoo, someone who'd
come here from someplace else. These customers almost
always got western designs—barbed-wire armbands, eagle
feathers with beads, cattle skulls, or a woman wearing a
holster, cowboy boots, and nothing else except a seductive
smile frozen mid-pucker next to a wisp of gunsmoke rising
from the business end of a revolver she was cuddling between her impossibly large breasts. Slade always did that
one because I hadn't mastered the art of making tattooed
hair look right.

By the time I started tattooing paying customers, tattooing was less about language and more about abstraction
and self-awareness. Even though the meanings had changed,
the images were still the same. It was as though a new language had been crafted from old, familiar words, easily
mistaken for one's native tongue.

I struggled with each tattoo, wondering how Slade
could make tattooing seem effortless. Every tattoo was a
lesson in placement, technique, and style. Eventually, it got
easier. I learned to stretch the really elastic parts, like the
small of the back or the bikini line—the small triangle of
flat skin framed by a hipbone, the curve of a belly, and a
pudendum. I learned to stretch arms from behind, pulling
the skin and muscle together in a big pinch until the front
of the arm was as taut as a drum.

I thought everything about the tattoo experience
should be exactly what the customer wanted. I let each one
browse through the CD collection and choose the music
we'd listen to while I tattooed. I let each one bring friends

into the tattoo room for moral support. In short, I let them make me crazy.

It was my fifth tattoo of the day, and the third time I'd listened to Metallica's *Kill 'Em All* in as many hours. My gloves were filled with perspiration, and the customers had whined about everything from the prices to the pain. The last customer of the day, Ron, wanted a Playboy bunny tattooed on his bikini line.

"Do you need me to take off my underwear?" Ron asked. "I can take off my underwear if it's necessary."

It was not necessary. Ron's friends crowded around us while I crouched in front of him, trying to place the stencil where it ought to go. "Stand straight," I said. "Put your weight evenly on both feet."

Ron shuffled over to the mirror, pants shackling his ankles, and examined the stencil from every possible angle. "What do you think?" He asked his friends. "Down a little bit?" They squatted and leaned to examine the purple stencil, nodding and grumbling.

I wiped off the stencil, reapplied the deodorant, and placed the Playboy bunny a fraction of an inch lower. This time, my efforts were met with pleased murmurs. I got Ron into the chair without ruining the stencil, folded a paper towel into Ron's underwear, and began the outline. The Metallica album was almost loud enough to drown out his whimpering, but there was no way to ignore the burgeoning erection pushing against Ron's underwear. I thought he'd be embarrassed, but he just winked and smiled at me while his friends chortled behind me.

I dipped the needles into the ink cup and pressed the foot pedal. I looked at Ron's smirky face and his nylon-covered hard-on. I got a good stretch on Ron's skin and touched the needles to his skin before I snapped. Without thinking twice, I flipped the top of the tattoo machine around as hard as I could, still tattooing, still doing my job, and holding on to the handgrip for all I was worth. The machine's electrical coils hit Ron's erection with a satisfying thwap that resulted in a howl of real pain.

When the tattoo was done, I gave Ron the Metallica album as a souvenir and he gave me a tip I couldn't decide whether or not I deserved. I went home, washed off the dark eyeliner I'd worn all day, and applied a coat of lipstick four shades lighter than the blackberry color to which I was accustomed. I pulled on a pair of black tights, even though it was the middle of July, and searched the back of my closet until I found a demure, long-sleeved pink floral dress that would hide my tattoos. My dishwater blond hair was dyed purple and cut punk short, except for my bangs, which hung in waves to my chin. They weren't actually *my* bangs; someone else's hair, dyed to match mine, was attached to the roots of my own with hot wax. The extensions had grown out a bit, creating an interesting blond dreadlock effect along the edge of my scalp.

I swept the bangs up and to one side, sprayed them into place, and checked the mirror. Between the makeup and the clothing, I'd come as close as I could to achieving what passed for normal in my family. I shook my head and sighed. Not close enough.

The minute I walked though their door, I became fourteen years old again. I felt my lower jaw harden into the sullen set face of me as a teenager, silently defying anyone to tell me what to do or not to do.

We sat down and ate supper. We all pretended that I wasn't tattooed, that I did something else for a living. I knew, though, that the suspension of disbelief could not last through an entire meal. I dreaded the moment when the conversation would turn from small talk to the topic of me, and I could smell it the way you can smell a storm coming when the wind is just right.

"Have you given any more thought to going back to school?" My father strained to keep a pleasant tone to his voice. "There's a wonderful library science program at the University of Texas. I have some catalogs and an application, if you're interested."

"I think I'll just work for a while, and then figure out what to do." I didn't look up.

"Are you still working with your friend?" My mother's question.

"Slade. Yes."

"Tattooing?"

"That's what we do there."

"And you, personally, are applying the pictures to people's skin?"

I nodded.

"Of course, you could stay in Laramie and go to UW." My father continued as though the tattoo interlude had never taken place. His train of thought was firmly on track. "If you do that, you really should think about buying a house. Paying rent isn't getting you anywhere, financially speaking. It's time to start thinking about building some credit for yourself."

"Do you really think that's a safe job?" My mother asked. "Will you even be able to support yourself?"

"It's perfectly safe, and I'll make plenty of money."

"Tattooing." My mother sighed.

"What?" My father's head swiveled in my direction.

"She's going to work for her friend in that tattoo parlor." My mother's cheerful smile segued into concern and disappointment.

"Megan Lowe is studying in Europe on a Fulbright scholarship." My father sighed deeply. "It's hard to believe that you used to baby-sit her. Isn't it? Doesn't seem like it was that long ago." He shook his head slightly and became intensely interested in pursuing a particular piece of roast beef around the plate with his fork. He gave up and put the fork down, looked at me, and sighed again.

The rest of dinner was a medley of strained sighs and awkward silences. After the dishwasher had been loaded and the good-byes had been said, I walked through the living room, with its white carpet and leather furniture, through the marble-tiled foyer. I felt like a trespasser.

My father was an optimistic man. For the conscious part of my twenty-six years—perhaps for the entirety of my twenty-six years—he had set forth realistic options and pragmatic career choices for me. Even after years of disappointments large and small, his ambitions for me were like a dangerous river, choppy and murky and fast. Occasionally, something in his river of sensible aspirations appealed to me, but I could never quite reach it; it floated by too quickly, too far from the banks. If I fell into the river, I'd be sucked under, drowning slowly while the current battered my head against submerged resentments and boulders of disillusion. If I was lucky, I'd wake up on a bank downstream, a midwestern librarian with a numbed artistic bent and no imagination.

The river of my own ambitions flowed into a brackish swamp.

There was a part of me that wanted more than anything to be like the rest of my family, to be the kind of person who'd have white carpet and cook roast beef for dinner. I would have liked to be the kind of person who would get excited at the prospect of a career in library science. Sometimes, I even would have liked to be the kind of person who wouldn't get tattooed, who wouldn't work in a tattoo parlor.

By 1990, tattooing was the only way I could make a living in Laramie, as an artist or otherwise. Over the course of the 1980s, Wyoming's overall population had declined, but Laramie's had remained a steady 27,000, more or less. The numbers were the same, but the faces were different. The price of real estate and rentals had climbed exponentially, and while people from other places found these prices reasonable, the children of Laramie's natives did not; there wasn't much to do, employment-wise, that paid anything close to a living wage. There were jobs to be had, but most were minimum-wage service-industry positions with little room for advancement, positions that were filled quickly by college students who were confident that they'd move on to something better after graduation.

Most of the kids I'd grown up with had moved away long before in search of cheaper costs of living or better jobs, and the few who hadn't left town were overeducated, underemployed, and living bitterly in mobile-home parks. I knew how lucky I was.

Rick's truck was in my driveway when I got home. Inside, Rick shifted his eyes away from the television long enough to acknowledge my presence as he lifted a bong to his lips and sucked in, long and hard, the flame crackling around the dried bud in the bowl above the frantic, angry sound of bubbling water.

"What are you wearing?" he asked without exhaling.

"I had dinner with my parents," I said.

"That can't be comfortable." Rick released a series of expanding smoke rings.

"What have you been doing?" I asked.

"Just watching TV." Rick tipped his head from side to side. "Thinking a little."

Rick's thinking was the flip side to his wildness, the wildness with which I had fallen in love, the wildness I assumed was kept in some sort of check by the integrity he tried to shrug off but couldn't shake. His wildness seemed less pure as time passed, and I'd come to realize that it stemmed from an uncontrollable lack of conscience that was deliciously nasty in bed, but dangerous in the real world.

The danger was like a drug, the adrenaline sensation of eluding the police or riding a fifty-year-old roller coaster notorious for its accidental-death toll or driving fast in a car with bad brakes or whatever thrill Rick thought up. I enjoyed flirting with death, the power of tiptoeing—or running, in most cases—right up to the edge and pulling back just before it was too late, even after I learned that the edge was always moving, that it might pop up sooner than expected. I learned that people have different limits for this sort of thing, and I pushed it hard, trying to find the place I'd stop before I got there, heart pounding, and say, *Enough is enough*. The price of admission to this particular theme park was putting up with Rick's thinking and a few other bad habits.

Rick was big on thinking. His head was like a lettuce spinner, leafy green thoughts plastered desperately to the edges of his mind, pushed away from the central vortex by centrifugal force, he said. Sometimes he drank to slow down the spin and grab at a thought, and sometimes it took something stronger. From the outside, it was hard to

believe he was deep in thought. Usually he was slumped on
the couch, syringe on the coffee table, eyes glued shut,
scratching a few days' worth of beard with one hand while
a Marlboro smoldered between the fingers of the other. It
looked like he was more likely to burn down the house
than to grab on to a thought and hold it, which is why I sat
and watched him.

Sometimes, when Rick was in a thinking mood, he
liked to ponder his elusive, leafy-green thoughts in the
bathtub and I'd have to watch him then, too, just in case his
head slipped under the water and didn't come back up.

That night, though, he'd only been thinking a little,
like he said, which just meant that we went to bed early
and I watched him sleep. I trailed my fingertips over the
roadmap of ink in his skin, remembering the first time I'd
touched him. After a while I mostly forgot that the tattoos
were even there, but at first his skin was the most erotic
and intimidating thing I'd ever seen. He had whirlpools on
his elbows, fish on his forearms, a demon on his belly, and
a monkey on his back. Skulls and stripes and dragons and
women. He had a flower here, a flower that I loved to
touch.

Rick liked everything about tattooing. He liked the ritual of the process, the finished product, the permanence.
Rick liked the pain. Whenever he was depressed, or sad or
angry or frustrated, there was nothing he liked better than
getting tattooed. The sting of the needles was a way of
translating his emotions into something physical. The pain
was a release, a physical manifestation of an ethereal ache,

and when the tattoo was finished and all healed up, it was another pretty picture, another badge. Another reminder.

Most of the time, his tattoos said more than he did. Even though Rick would answer any question honestly, voluntary information about his life was dispensed on a need-to-know basis, the criteria for which was murky and glittering with contradictions.

In the morning, Rick came out of the shower and said, "Gotta give my brother a ride today. You want to come with?"

"You have a brother?" I asked.

Rick nodded.

"Sure," I said.

We got into his truck and headed west on I-80. I'd kind of thought Rick's brother needed a ride from one place in Laramie to another, but I didn't say anything. I sat back and watched the scenery unfold, miles and miles of sparse grass and sagebrush, tumbleweeds and angled wooden snow fence, zinc-colored ponds and glistening patches of dry soda. Somewhere around Elk Mountain, curiosity got the best of me.

"Where are we going?" I asked.

"Rawlins."

"Your brother lives in Rawlins?"

"He did," Rick said, "for a while. He gets out today."

"Oh." Even though Rawlins suffered an unusually heavy air of quiet desperation, "getting out" wasn't what most people there called moving away. The Wyoming State Penitentiary is just outside of town.

Travis was ready to go when we pulled up at the guarded entrance. We parked in plain view, and he walked from the administration building to the truck. Travis was tall and slim, built like Rick, but that was the only resemblance I could find. Travis's head was set low on a bandanna-ringed neck, and the collar of his shirt rose to meet the sloping brim of his cowboy hat. The hat was worn and creased, curved low over his forehead and stained by rain and sweat. His lower lip was pushed out over a wad of chewing tobacco, and his face was so tanned and weathered that it might have been cut from a piece of saddle leather.

He tossed a duffel bag into the back of the truck and opened the door. When I slid over to make room, he touched the brim of his hat, gave me a little nod and part of a smile.

"Hey," Rick said.

"Hey."

There was a long silence.

"Got paroled," Travis said. "That means you can start up the truck and get me out of here as quickly as possible. Obeyin' the speed limit laws, 'course."

Rick laughed and peeled out of the parking lot. He drove back toward Rawlins and stopped before he got to the I-80 interchange.

"You hungry?" Rick asked. "Or do you just want to get the hell out of Dodge?"

"Hungry, yeah. Anything to get the taste of prison food out of my mouth."

Rick crossed the interstate, found the frontage road, and turned into the McDonald's drive-thru.

"Hey, man," Travis said, "this is prison food. They just serve it faster."

Rick laughed and drove around the building, eased into traffic, and drove west. "You pick it, man. My treat."

"Head on down by the tracks," Travis said. "Ought to be something decent there."

Rick cruised the numbered streets and finally found a diner with a faded sign and gingham curtains in the window. Travis had the door open and was standing on the curb before the truck had even come to a complete stop.

It was after lunch and before supper and we were the only customers. There was a counter in the back with round stools, and the walls were lined with Formica-topped booths and worn leatherette benches beneath a wall covered with hand-lettered signs that advertised the specials. We slid into a booth.

The cook was pulling double-duty waiting tables. The pin on her uniform said Marge. Her hair was teased sky-high and dyed an impossible auburn, and when she leaned over to arrange silverware and menus, she dosed us with the smell of Juicy Fruit gum. She smiled big and poured coffee without being asked.

"What can I bring you?"

"Grilled cheese sandwich," I said, "and fries."

"Chicken-fried steak, please," Rick said. "You serve beer?"

"Pick your poison," Marge laughed.

"Long-neck Bud, if you've got it."

Travis was hunkered over his menu like he wanted one of everything.

"You know what you want, Hon?" Marge asked.

"Could I taste the gravy?" Travis asked.

"What?"

"I'm thinking on having a chicken-fried, too," Travis said, "but I was wondering if I could taste the gravy first. Gravy says a lot about a place, you know."

"You got that right," Marge laughed. She shoved her pencil into her hair. "Bring your spoon, Hon."

He picked up his spoon and followed Marge into the kitchen, his bootheels popping on the linoleum floor. When Travis came back, he brushed his hand against the nape of my neck, gently pulling my shirt away from the dragon tattoo that had been peeking out. "How far down does that one go?"

"Have some decorum," Rick said. "That's my old lady. Keep your hands to yourself."

Travis apologized and sat down. "What's it like to be a chick and be all tattooed like that?"

"I don't know what it's like to not be a chick and not be all tattooed," I said. "I think it's pretty much the same, though."

"You getting a chicken-fried?" Rick asked.

"Two. That's some damn fine gravy. Where you from?" Travis asked me.

"Laramie," I said.

"Lookin' like that?" He waved his spoon up and down. "What do you do?"

"She works for Slade," Rick said. "Tattooing."

"Huh." Travis said. "There much call for that sort of thing?"

"Enough, I guess," I said. "The shop's been there for five years."

Rick had finished his first beer and started on his second when Marge brought our food out. She balanced a round tray on one hip and slid our plates onto the table.

"What's there to do for work in town?" Travis asked. He cut through a double-decker chicken-fried steak and dragged a forkful of gravy-drenched meat through his mashed potatoes.

"Construction, mostly," Rick said. "We got a Wal-Mart now, if you want to work indoors."

"No shit?"

"Yeah. You're not gonna believe town. It's all cowboyed up, and expensive as hell, too."

"Bound to happen sooner or later. No one to blame but ourselves, really," Travis said.

"I didn't do anything," I said.

"Me either," Rick said, around a mouthful of mixed vegetables.

"Not us as in you, me, and the tattoo chick, but us like the West in general. Man, how long have people here been pimping an image for tourist dollars? You got Jubilee Days, Frontier Days, whatever, people and towns dressed up to look like what the tourists expect, sooner or later they're gonna want to move here. As long as someone's putting on a show that matches the John Wayne movies in their minds, they think there's always gonna be a frontier." Travis looked at my grilled cheese. "Can I have a bite?"

"Sure," I said.

He picked up half of the sandwich, dunked it in his gravy, and took a big bite. When he handed it back, the half circle of the bite he'd taken was etched with the imprint of his teeth and ringed with gravy. I went ahead and finished it; Travis was right—it was damn fine gravy, and possibly the best grilled cheese sandwich I'd ever had.

"It's the way they act, though," Rick said, "like they can come out here and rearrange everything how they want it, even though, when it comes right down to it, the frontier isn't a piece of land or even a state of mind. All it is now is the moment between knowing that you have to make a choice and actually picking one thing over something else. The only frontier anyone's got anymore is that split second when all your options are still open." He reached over and plundered a handful of my French fries. "Want some mashed potatoes?" he asked.

"No, that's okay." I looked at Travis. "Plus, too," I said, "Laramie was already settled."

"Hell, it was already settled the first time," Travis said. "It already belonged to someone else. One man's frontier is almost always another man's backyard. Besides, if it weren't for them, I bet you couldn't make a living pokin' pictures on people."

"If it weren't for them, I could make a living doing something else, though," I said.

"Hey," Travis shrugged. "There's nothing more American than taking over."

"You all want dessert?" Marge refilled my coffee cup and set another Budweiser in front of Rick.

"You got apple pie?" Travis asked.

"Apple, cherry, key lime, peach, and maybe a piece of chocolate."

"Apple," Travis said.

"You want to taste it first, or you want a whole piece?" Marge asked.

"I trust you," Travis said. "May as well bring the whole piece."

"May as well bring the whole pie," Rick said. "It'll get eaten."

Luckily, it was only half a pie. Marge served it in its pan and set a stack of forks and plates next to it.

"Pie was as good as the gravy," Travis told Marge as she calculated our bill on an ancient cash register. Rick paid and tipped big.

"Thanks," Marge said. "You all come back soon."

"If this place wasn't in Rawlins," Travis said, "I'd eat here every day."

We piled into the truck and got back on the interstate.

I'd thought Travis needed a ride back to Laramie, so I was surprised when Rick turned off on Highway 130, which goes through Saratoga and Encampment. He drove

south for a long time. The sun shone sideways across the
craggy profile of the mountains. Accordion pleats of lime-
stone jutted out, prominent ridges along jagged, shadowy
crevices where runoff and erosion gutted rock and dirt.
Rimrock bones thrust upward from a collar of pine trees
and alluvial debris, topped with a brow ridge of Precam-
brian crystalline boulders whose recesses were filled with
year-round snow, blue gray in the shadows.

Rick made a hasty turn onto an unmarked road that
was pocked and cracked. The asphalt lasted a mile before
it turned into gravel that turned into dirt so quickly that I
thought he might have made a wrong turn. The sun slid
down the back of the mountains behind a veil of moody
gray clouds, and the wind picked up, stirring the dust on the
road. Tumbleweeds caught under the chassis, scraping along
until they popped free behind the truck. Luminous drops of
rain began to fall, intermittent at first, and then plopping
hard and fast onto the windshield. Rick stuck his hand out
the window, shivered, and flipped on the windshield wipers
and the heater. He started to roll up his window.

"Hey, don't," Travis reached across me and touched
Rick's arm. "It smells like freedom out there."

The road twisted toward a ranch at the base of the
mountains. Yellow-green hills sprinkled with sage fell into
the horizon on either side of the buildings, the whole thing
framed by a yawning, gunmetal sky.

Rick eased the truck over the washboard ruts. He slowed
when the road forked and pulled onto the less-traveled of

the two prongs, which was marked with a wagon-wheel-flanked cattle guard and a crooked wooden sign warning against the uninvited.

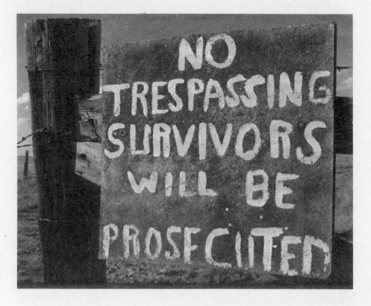

A ranch house and a barn were clustered with an assortment of outbuildings against the side of the mountain, half a mile or so away. The lights were on inside, cozy yellow against the weather and trespassing sentiments, and the idea of people living all the way out here in this hard beauty caused my throat to tighten until I was blinking back tears for no real reason. Travis got out, grabbed his duffel bag from the bed of the truck, and leaned inside to shake Rick's hand. "Hey, Bro, does the chick have more tattoos than you do?"

"I don't know," Rick said. "I never counted. But I bet she does." He shook his brother's hand again, and we watched Travis walk up the lane.

"Who lives there?" I asked.

"My folks."

"Wow," I said. "It's beautiful."

"Used to be." Rick said. "Now it just seems like a dead person who used to laugh a lot."

He backed the truck into the lane and turned it around. We took the back way home, over the Snowy Range, past glacial lakes, through Centennial.

"What'd he do?" I asked. We could see the lights of Laramie.

"Travis? 'Bout half of a three-to-five."

"No, I mean, what did he do to get there?" I asked.

"He had this girlfriend, this pretty little blue-eyed gal who waited tables out at Woods Landing. She had this beat-up old Rambler that she drove to work every day, and the tires were so bald she kept sliding off into the borrow pit every time it snowed. Travis was rodeoing up by Gillette, and one night he was all liquored up and got to thinking about his girl's tires, and somehow he got it in his head that it'd be chivalrous to fetch her some new ones. So he saddled up his horse and rode over to the Big O tire store downtown and heaved a cinder block through the window, setting off all kinds of alarms. He rode off with a brand-new Pirelli under each arm, which was a bit conspicuous, even in Gillette. The cops caught up to him before he even got back to the fairgrounds. Had to pay to fix the window, and didn't get to keep the tires, 'course."

"That's the most romantically stupid story I've ever heard," I said. "I can't believe he'd get three-to-five for that."

"It seems he'd also stashed a healthy amount of methamphetamine in his saddle bags. Cops found it when they searched the horse."

"I wouldn't have thought speed and cowboys went together," I said.

"Hey," he shrugged. "It's Wyoming, not *Bonanza*."

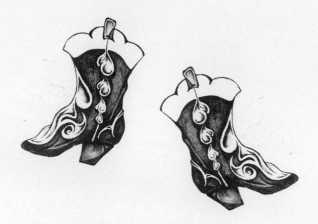

Chapter Six

"Pɪᴄᴋ ᴏᴜᴛ sᴏᴍᴇᴛʜɪɴɢ for your thigh," Slade said. I'd been working in the shop for more than a year. My apprenticeship had ended a long time ago, but Slade was wearing his teacher face.

"Why?" I asked.

"You'll be tattooing yourself this evening," he said.

"Why?"

"Because you asked why. That, right there, is your answer. You need to know exactly what you're doing to other people when you pick up a tattoo machine."

"I'm plenty tattooed," I said. "I know what it feels like."

"You know how it feels when someone else tattoos you, but you don't know how it feels when you tattoo."

"Oh." I felt small and slightly ashamed. "Do I do it wrong? Is my hand too heavy?"

"No. But this is a big step toward becoming a tattoo artist instead of a hack. It will always be there, in the back of your mind, how a tattoo machine in your hand feels to the person you're tattooing."

I spent the morning drawing and erasing and drawing some more. Drawing something—anything—for a customer was easy, but drawing my own tattoo was impossible. Any flaw, even a small one that meant nothing on paper, would be something I'd have to look at on my leg for the rest of my life. I browsed through the file cabinet full of flash designs, even though I didn't want a tattoo that anyone else had. I spent the afternoon looking through books and finally found a picture of a chrysanthemum. When I showed it to Slade, he nodded like it didn't matter one way or another, like the design wasn't as important as the experience. It was a very small chrysanthemum in the book, so I enlarged the drawing until it was big enough to wrap around the top of my thigh. I assembled my liner machine and waited for the stencil to dry.

Slade stuck his head around the doorway and pointed at my thigh. "What the hell is that?"

"The chrysanthemum I showed you," I said.

"Yeah, I can see that. But wasn't it, oh, I don't know, about twenty times smaller?"

"Look at my leg," I said. "You're the one who explained placement to me. That tattoo would look horrible the size it was, just floating in the middle of all that empty space."

"I know, but this is a mental exercise. You don't have to torture yourself."

"I don't want it small." I could feel my lower lip sticking out stubbornly.

"Suit yourself." Slade started to put his coat on just as I was assembling my liner machine.

"Where are you going?" I asked. I didn't want to admit that I was more than a little bit scared to tattoo myself without him somewhere nearby, just in case I couldn't do it.

"Meeting Rick at the Buckhorn for a beer." Slade laughed at the look on my face. "Don't worry. I'll come back and check on you." He locked the door on his way out.

After five minutes of outlining, I wished I'd stenciled the chrysanthemum smaller. Much, much smaller. The act of tattooing and the act of getting tattooed seemed to be diametrically opposed. When I was tattooing someone else, I concentrated on stretching the skin, needle depth, solid color. When I was being tattooed, I concentrated on accepting and releasing the pain, on sitting still, on the permanence of the ink and how I'd feel about it after it healed. It was difficult to do both these things at once. When I thought only about technique, it hurt more than I'd imagined possible, and when I tried to deal with the sensation, I couldn't keep the needles at a consistent depth.

After an hour or so, I heard Slade's key in the lock. He and Rick came into the tattoo room, and I was hoping neither of them would look too closely at the outline I'd done.

"Want some help?"

I shook my head and tattooed along the stencil line of the top petal. My eyes watered. "Maybe," I said.

Rick sat on the edge of the counter while Slade finished up the outline of the chrysanthemum, and it went much faster with the machine in Slade's hand instead of my own. When the needles edged toward the inside of my thigh, my leg began to twitch and I bit my lip. Rick reached over and placed a steady hand on my arm. "Pain don't hurt," he said. "Remember that."

THE BODY ART WORKSHOP was a three-room, L-shaped space. The front door opened into a waiting area with storefront windows, a plush couch, a coffee table, and flash-covered walls. The table and couch were covered, as often as not, with photographs of tattoos we'd done, drawings of tattoos we were going to do, and tattoo magazines. A short hallway ended with saloon-style swinging doors that led into the tattoo room. A window between the tattoo area and the waiting room let potential customers watch while we worked, but could be closed off with venetian blinds for privacy. Sometimes we closed the blinds just because it got to be too much: *What are you getting? How much does a tattoo cost? How many tattoos do you have?* Slade drew up a cartoon balloon and taped it to our side of the window. Inside, it said "Does it hurt?" Every time someone leaned through the window to take a good, long look at us while we worked, the balloon hung above their heads, the ever-present question.

Tattooing borrows from many other art forms — drawing and painting, of course, but sculpture, too. In technical terms, a tattoo is an image on an elastic form, like a picture on a balloon. It changes as the body moves, grows or shrinks, gets older. Some tattoos take on three-dimensional qualities as a result of the underlying muscle structure, and some tattoos, especially large ones, can be viewed only in sections. It's like sculpture that way.

Tattooing anything on human skin felt like art at first, but after I mastered the technical aspects of tattooing, the novelty wore off. I wanted to put my skills to more aesthetic use than, say, the twenty-five-dollar rose, but convincing the customers that tattooing had possibilities beyond the flash on the walls was difficult.

Other forms of art were entirely solitary pursuits, which was great for creativity but left me floundering for direction when it came to turning creativity into a career. Tattooing was different, a collaboration between artist and canvas, and while I made a career out of it, at times I missed non-living forms of art. A photograph never once said, "Oh, ow, I have to take a break," when it was in the developer tray. A camera never spoke up to say it thought the image might look better a little to the left. My oil palette never tried to convince me to listen to a homemade recording of thrash-metal grunge songs that the pigments had produced in their parents' garage.

FRANKIE WAS A TALL, gawky boy with gangly legs and a sincere smile who had affected the habit of wearing baggy shorts that had once been large-waisted pants, cut off with a hunting knife and cinched at the waist. He'd come to the University of Wyoming from a ranch in eastern Montana and reinvented himself, trading his horse for a skateboard, but there was no disguising the cowboy walk, the way his legs looped outward at the knees while his feet swung gracefully in a straight line.

Frankie's first tattoo was a Celtic design on his calf. He came into the shop clutching a drawing on a rumpled piece of paper, looked at the flash on the walls, and folded the paper in quarters before I could see what it was. He looked at the flash carefully, unfolded the paper, and folded it up again. He looked at more flash. He unfolded and refolded the paper.

"How much for this one?" He pointed at a Celtic piece on the wall.

"Hundred and sixty," I said. "Can I see your drawing?"

He hemmed and hawed and bobbed his head from side to side before he took the crumpled piece of paper out of his pocket. It was a Celtic design that was similar to the flash piece, but way better. It was symmetrical, for starters.

"Why don't you get this one?" I pointed to the drawing.

"I'm not a real artist," he said. "Can you do it now?"

I handed him a release form on a clipboard and a pen.

Asking what made an artist real would only have made things worse. Besides, I already knew. His drawing wasn't hanging on the wall, hadn't been bought for such a display by a tattoo shop. It wasn't laminated. It wasn't signed or numbered. I thought about the chrysanthemum I'd tattooed on my thigh.

I finished Frankie's tattoo in two sittings, one for the outline and shading and another for the color, and tattooed him again, a month or so later, outlining a red-and-black Tlinglit fish that would take at least a year to finish. The tail wrapped around the top of his foot and the fish circled his entire leg, and the head took up most of his thigh. When he walked, the whole thing rippled.

Eventually not a day went by without Frankie's presence in the shop, whether he had an appointment or not. He'd bring a friend he wanted me to meet. He'd bring a tape he wanted me to hear. He'd stop by just to say hello, unmindful that the tattoo shop was where I worked, and as with any other job, I had work to do. Even if there wasn't a customer in the chair, there were custom designs to draw, stencils to make, needles to solder, or books to keep.

I could have put a stop to it, but I didn't. By then, Frankie was letting me tattoo pretty much whatever I wanted, wherever I thought it would look best, and he was paying me to do it, every other week. In between sessions of Tlinglit fish coloring, I used techniques from other media, experimenting with negative space and chiaroscuro and diluted inks like watercolor washes. I tattooed a snowflake on Frankie's shoulder blade. Instead of a black outline, I began with lavender, tattooing just inside the stencil line so that the needles wouldn't push the dark purple stencil ink into the skin and darken the lavender pigment. I filled it in with concentrated white tinged with frosty blues that warmed to a pale purple at the edges. When it was healed, the tattoo was faint, almost invisible, but anything that reddened the surrounding skin—sun, sauna, a hot shower—caused the snowflake to reappear.

The snowflake was followed by a spiral design flowing from a silhouetted tree in the center of Frankie's back. The spiral began like tight bicycle spokes, dark and heavy colors, thin lines that widened as the spiral fanned out, flowing into green and blue washes that faded away altogether. The skin between the spiral's coil looked raised and rounded. Negative space.

ONE EVENING IN JUNE, I stopped by the shop around closing time. It was my day off and I didn't need to be there, but I'd promised Slade dinner and a movie. When I walked into the tattoo room, a woman was lying in the tattoo chair. She wasn't wearing pants. Slade was tattooing a butterfly on the side of her hip.

"Oh," I said. "Sorry." I backed into the front room.

"Hang on!" The buzzing of the tattoo machine stopped. Slade hurried into the front room. "Come on back and talk to me. I'm bored."

"Really?" I raised my eyebrows and tipped my head toward the tattoo room. It was difficult to believe that a half-naked woman with a flirty smile would be something Slade might find boring, but he made a face and nodded. "She's here for *all* the wrong reasons," he whispered. "And she won't sit still. Her name is Misty."

Misty's flirty smile narrowed ever so slightly when I pulled up a chair. "How many tattoos do you have?" she asked.

"None." I lied because it was my day off, lied because I was tired of talking to tattoo customers, lied because I didn't want a single thing in common with Misty.

"This is my third." She looked at me as though she had one up on me in the race for Slade's affections, and I thought about telling her that she had two up on me, seeing as how Slade didn't want to date me any more than I wanted to date him. Then she smirked, and suddenly I wasn't feeling charitable.

"A lot of times," Slade said, "one tattoo leads to another. Most people who get a second tattoo put more time and thought into design and placement, and that second tattoo is almost always better than the first. If you get two tattoos, it's easy to get a third. This time, you've got a better handle on the whole thing. Most people pick the design first, for a change, and then figure out the best possible place on their bodies to put it. Almost always, you like your third tattoo the best."

I glanced at Misty's half-finished tattoo and wondered what her other tattoos might look like, especially if what Slade was saying was true. The butterfly was just flash, nothing special. It wasn't even the best flash butterfly we had.

"They say you can stop at three," Slade went on. "That might be true. They say, too, that the fourth tattoo is the turning point. No reason to stop at four, maybe that's how the reasoning goes. Maybe it's just wanting the adrenaline high. What do you think, Misty?"

"I don't know," she said. "I never really thought about it. I get tattoos to mark certain milestones in my life, so I can look at them and think about how far I've come."

I sat back and opened a tattoo magazine, listening to Slade talk as he worked. He'd been telling me bits and pieces of tattoo lore for years, teaching me little by little since the day we'd met. My apprenticeship was all about the craft, just like any other tattoo apprenticeship; it's not like I was ever tested on the obscure facts of pre-technological tattooing among extinct cultures or any of the other tattoo tangents that Slade had explained in such great detail they seemed more like esoteric knowledge than trivia. Despite a tendency to present his opinions as hard facts, a propensity to infuse sketchy details with conjectured meaning, and his impatience when I couldn't keep up with the full-steam zigzag logic whenever his train of thought derailed without slowing down, Slade wove the past and present of tattooing through everything he knew or imagined when it came to the *whys* and *hows* of other people and other cultures. Slade was the kind of person who liked to know where things came from, how things worked. He liked history. Background.

"Until the 1960s, tattooing was basically a working man's art form—emphasis on the *man* part. Then everything changed. The Tattoo Renaissance, they call it. These guys were influenced by the Japanese traditional tattoos— bright colors and large images, lots of water or clouds or flowers—that follow the curves of a person's body." Slade paused to spritz the tattoo with green soap. He wiped away the excess ink and blood and checked his work carefully. Misty winced. She brightened up when Slade started talking again, but when it was still tattoo talk, she looked bored.

"Then Janis Joplin got a tattoo, and pretty much all of a sudden, tattooing wasn't just for sailors and bikers, wasn't just for guys." Slade put down the tattoo machine and rubbed the kinks out of his hands. "And now you've got MTV and a generation of would-be rebels, and suddenly tattoos are cool." Slade picked up the machine, adjusted the rheostat, and went back to work. "People who wouldn't have been caught dead in a tattoo parlor are rushing right in. Take Misty here, for example."

"What?" Misty asked.

"Goddamnit." Slade's head was down; she couldn't see his smile, but I could.

"What?" She twisted her torso and tried to jerk her leg out of his grasp to see what had happened.

"Don't worry," he said. "I can fix it. I'm almost positive I can fix it."

"What? What is it?"

Slade laughed. "My favorite joke. Gets 'em every time." Misty forced a smile and a giggle. "I would have just died if you'd been serious," she said. "This is the most important tattoo I've ever gotten."

I thought maybe I was wrong, maybe it wasn't the same butterfly Slade and I tattooed four or five times a week, in various sizes and different colors, a butterfly off the sheet of flash hanging at eye-level closest to the door. I leaned over my tattoo magazine to take a better look, to see what I must have missed. Nothing. It was the same old butterfly, this time in shades of mauve and purple.

"It's a symbol of beauty and freedom," Misty said. "It's about how I've finally become my own person."

"If you want to be more literal about it," Slade said, "it's something that starts out as a worm, something with a very short life span, something that ends up splattered on the grille of somebody's car if it's not eaten by a bird first."

FRIDAY WAS Delta Tau Delta day in the shop. All the new pledges were expressing their eternal devotion to a fraternity they'd just joined by having the house's crest tattooed on their ankles.

I was packed into the tattoo room with eight other people and the first customer. He'd asked if he could put in a CD he'd brought, and since he seemed extra-nervous, I let him do it, regretting this decision from the very first note. The tattoo shop was awash in bad dance music. The air was heavy with the smell of green soap, body heat, and other people's breath. A fan in the corner oscillated behind the crowd, but the breeze it generated was fetid and moist by the time it reached my face.

The young man in the chair was twitchy and full of *ow, ouch, ow's* before I even touched his skin with the needles. I leaned over his ankle, stretched the skin away from the bone, and began to tattoo. His leg flew up, and even though I sensed it coming in time to pull the tattoo machine back, I couldn't get my head out of the way in time. His foot caught my chin hard, and that's when Slade walked in. He came into the tattoo room and started pointing his finger.

"You, you, and you—all of you, actually—go out there."

"They can stay," the boy in the chair said.

"We're all going to take a little break," Slade said.

I unclipped the power cord and peeled off my gloves while my tattoo-in-progress limped in the direction his friends had gone.

"Hang on," Slade said. "Come back over here and sit down."

"Thanks." He sank gratefully onto my stool. "I was starting to feel lightheaded or something."

"I think customer service is very important," Slade said. "I do. Even in a tattoo shop. Maybe especially in a tattoo shop. But, especially in a tattoo shop, the customer is not always right. You need to accept this and decide what's going to happen next."

"What?" He looked at Slade uncertainly.

"This is not my music. This is not Karol's music. So I'm guessing that you brought your own music, right? Is that something you normally take to a place of business? Do you go to the Buckhorn and ask them to unplug the jukebox so that you can listen to the music you brought? No. But here we are, listening to your CD, even though Karol doesn't share your fondness for techno."

"You don't like techno?" His attention turned toward me for all the wrong reasons. "You must not have been listening to the right stuff. This band kicks ass. Just listen to it—really listen, all the way to the end—and I bet you'll change your mind. The beat's more than just rhythm. You can feel it."

"This is not about techno," Slade said. "This is about choices and consequences. Karol's job is to tattoo people. That's why she's got the machine with all the needles and these little bottles of ink. Her job is to make sure that your tattoo looks good. Part of that is making sure that you're comfortable, which must be why my stereo speakers are cranking out this shit. And you must have looked a little nervous when you asked if your friends could watch, so I guess Karol must have said, 'Sure, the more the merrier.'"

"It hurts, though," he said. "It really hurts."

"I know. Pretty much everybody knows it hurts," Slade said.

"It hurts more than I thought it would, though."

"Look at your leg," Slade said. "The purple part? That's stencil. It washes off. The black is tattoo ink." Slade pointed at a half-inch squiggle. "And it's not even deep enough to last. It's your choice. You can stop right now, or you can let her finish your tattoo. But if you want her to keep working, you've got to decide what part of the next hour is the most important to you, the tattoo or the experience of getting it."

"What do you mean? I'm supposed to pretend it doesn't hurt?"

"No," Slade said, "you just have to sit still even though it does hurt, assuming that a good tattoo is more important to you than the experience of getting tattooed. If it's somehow more exciting to watch her try to tattoo a straight line at a consistent depth on your leg while it's moving, that's something altogether different. Of course, the tattoo is going to suck big time, and Karol and I are both going to feel kind of bad, but that's where customer service interferes with our artistic goals. You paid up front, so you can make this experience whatever you want it to be. And yeah, if you play the whole thing up, you'll have a wild story to tell. At the end of it, you can point to the tattoo, the one that's going to suck, and you don't even have to talk about how you wouldn't sit still. You can sigh real big and shake your head and talk about how you'll never get tattooed again, wouldn't have gotten this one if you'd known now what you'll know by then. Maybe you'll get lucky and your leg will spaz straight up again while she's tattooing, only this time maybe she won't see it coming and you'll have some interesting scar tissue where you skewered yourself on the needles. That way, you can talk about how it took forever to heal up. But sooner or later, the story is going to grow old, or you'll run out of people to tell it to, and then where will you be?"

"I don't know."

"I don't know either," Slade said, "but wherever you are, you'll have a bad tattoo keeping you company. Now, you can either sit down and sit still and let Karol do her job, or you can get the hell out. Either way, that fucking music has *got* to go."

Chapter Seven

$\mathcal{B}$Y 1991, WYOMING'S ranches were being parceled out to the highest bidder. Selling off a few acres of perimeter pasture to make ends meet wasn't new, but it was usually a last, grudging resort for most ranchers, a way of cheating the bank man out of a foreclosure note. Subdividing was something else altogether; heritage seemed like it ought to be tucked away in the "everything" people say that money can't buy.

Many of these ranches, pretty or not, weren't even for sale at first. If, say, someone was a third-generation rancher and his or her father died, the ranch might be appraised at "development" value, which meant that a $100,000 spread could be assessed at ten million dollars. While cattle were selling for sixty cents a pound, this same someone would be expected to pay estate taxes of about five million dollars—not for what the land was, but for what it could be—and most third-generation ranchers didn't have five million dollars. Sometimes they sold the whole spread (usually for far less than the appraised value) and moved away. Sometimes, especially around the Tetons and Jackson Hole, they sold their inheritances to someone rich, someone from someplace else, and signed on as hired hands.

Rick's father had been staving off the inevitable by allowing tourists to stay in the bunkhouse and take part in day-to-day ranch life. He'd been talked into this venture by a loan officer at his bank, who'd been talked into it by a travel agent from Laramie. The ranch was somewhere between "working" and "dude," with a gloomy future.

IT WAS ONE MORE thing Rick didn't mention, and when he did, I had to piece the details together from his ambiguous answers to one direct question after another. He and Slade and I were in his truck at the time, on the way to the ranch, and it took me most of the two-hour drive to pry the story loose. None of us was exactly what you'd call an early riser; the tattoo shop opened at noon, which meant Slade and I stayed up late and slept in later. Rick, too, kept what he liked to call his "own hours," most of which didn't involve direct sunlight.

The day before, Rick had picked me up at work. As an afterthought, almost, he asked, "Either of you know how to ride?"

"Horses?" Slade asked.

"Yeah," I said. "Why?"

"My dad broke his leg, and there's some cattle to move this weekend. On the ranch."

"You come from a ranch?" Slade clapped his hands over his mouth, faking horrified surprise.

"Yeah." Rick looked at Slade like he was daring him to laugh.

"Right on," Slade said.

Slade taped a note to the front door of the shop, explaining that we'd be closed all day on Saturday, the busiest day of the week, due to the unforeseen circumstances of a family emergency. Rick smiled then.

We left Laramie at four o'clock on Saturday morning and drove two hours in the dark, turning onto the ranch lane just as the sun was peeking over the mountains. Rick introduced us to his father, who was sitting on the wooden steps that led up to the porch, holding a knife and a piece of green aspen, one leg encased in a plaster cast, propped up on a wobbly kitchen chair.

"Nice to meet you, Mr. Edwards." I smiled and stuck out my hand.

"Real fancy manners for a gal with purple hair and pictures all over herself. Might as well call me Marvin. Those real?" Marvin pointed at the tattoos on my arm.

"Nah. She paints 'em on every morning," Slade said. Marvin laughed out loud and slapped his thigh. The screen door creaked open behind him, and Travis stuck his head out.

"Can I talk to you for a minute, Bro?" Travis twitched his head toward the side of the house and began walking without waiting for an answer. Slade and I followed Rick.

Travis leaned back against the side of the house and pulled one leg up, resting the sole of his boot on the log wall. He was wearing a saucer-sized western belt buckle, and it wasn't the kind you could buy. It was a buckle you had to hurt yourself besting an animal and beating time to get.

"The guests ain't happy," Travis said. "They're not having an experience. There's nothing to do. There ain't any organized activities, and they say Pop's not being nice. The cook forgot to take the skin off the chicken before it got fried, and there was only two breasts. Rest was dark meat." Travis made languid quotation marks with his fingers when he said "experience," "do," "activities," "nice," and "forgot."

"The cook?" Rick asked. "You mean Mom?"

"Yep. Last night they started grumbling about wanting some of their money back, being as how this isn't what they expected on a real ranch."

"Give it back, then," Slade said. "Tell 'em not to let the state line hit 'em on the ass."

"Can't," Travis said. "The money's spent. Pop was behind on the payments."

"For what?" Rick asked.

"Everything."

"What are you going to do?" I asked.

"I thought up an experience," Travis said, "but I need some help."

Ten minutes later, we were upstairs in Rick and Travis's childhood bedroom, trying on pants and trading boots, tossing our rejects onto the knotty-pine bunk beds. We were all wearing Marvin's old rodeo shirts, all loud colors and unfamiliar tailoring. Mine was green with big red and yellow flowers embroidered on the yoke and three bright red snaps on the very long cuff of each sleeve. The row of matching snaps down the front looked like Christmas-tree lights against the green fabric. The shirt was tucked into a pair of Travis's old Wranglers, and I was wearing a pair of brown Tony Lama boots that had been Rick's when he was a teenager. We picked out our own hats. Rick's was a worn brown Stetson with a floppy brim, and Slade had a new, black, 10x beaver-felt Resistol that Travis hadn't gotten around to breaking in yet. Mine was the color of butter and soft, with a sweat-stained band and the lingering scent of a long-forgotten cowboy's pomade.

Travis came in for a final inspection, nodded at Rick, shoved a can of chewing tobacco into the back pocket of Slade's borrowed Wranglers, and looked at me. His face scrunched up funny and he shook his head. "You can't have purple hair," Travis said.

"But I do," I said. "I do have purple hair."

"Stay right there; can't take a chance on the guests seeing you like that." A few minutes later, we could hear the sounds of Travis's boots on the attic floor above our heads, lots of stomping and rummaging and heavy things being tossed about. He came back breathless and dusty, holding a package wrapped in brown paper. He unrolled it carefully and held up a wig, long black hair in two thick braids wrapped with strips of leather that had feathers tucked into the knots.

"That's better than purple?" Slade asked.

"You haven't met the guests," Travis said. "This is perfect."

I sat on the bottom bunk while Travis tried to tug the wig onto my head.

"Not only is it purple," he said, "there's way too much of it." He looked down at the sheathed knife on his belt.

"No," I said. "No way. You are not cutting my hair."

Travis sighed and everyone took turns shoving strands

of my hair under the wig. When it was done, the four of us stood in front of the mirror. Travis looked like a cowboy, but the rest of us looked like extras on the set of a low-budget, surreal western movie. Rick and Slade collapsed against each other, laughing until tears rolled down their cheeks, and I just stood there, looking at my mirrored self, holding a feathered braid in each hand.

"The guests won't know the difference," Travis said.

We filed downstairs. The kitchen was filled with the sounds of rattling dishes and bacon sizzle, and the smells of breakfast mixed with the smells of summer that floated in through the open windows. I was instantly, ravenously, hungry. Rick's mother, Rose, dropped her spoon and clapped both hands over her mouth, giggling, when she saw us. Rose was shaped like a fertility fetish, the round shelf of her butt mirrored by a matching protrusion of belly and a rolling bosom upon which her chins were stacked like saucers. She had a small, pretty face with a pert nose and cherubic lips, and her flashing hazel eyes were wide and round. There was a whole lot of her, but it was all beautiful.

"You do something to your hair?" Rick asked

"Had Dottie cut it." Rose smiled. "And I curled it a bit. You like it?"

"Looks great," Travis said. "New outfit, too?"

I looked at the stiff, tight jeans that Rose must have struggled to zip, topped with a flowered blouse that gaped at the buttons across her bosom. Rose's feet were bunched into a pair of beige flats, her flesh reddening where the shoes pushed against her pudgy feet.

"Ordered it all off that shopping channel on the TV," Rose said. "Sizes seem to run small, but I did want something new to wear today. First day of summer and all."

"Lookin' good, Mom." Rick hugged her and began to set the table.

We went out to the porch and sat down with Marvin while Travis ambled toward the bunkhouse. Marvin picked up the knife and the aspen branch and resumed his whittling. "More trouble than they're worth," he said. "Can't teach 'em to rope for shit. Goddamn shame you can take the beef out of ranching and make more money off pretend cowboys than you ever could with a decent herd." Marvin slid the knife beneath the bark. "They're from San Diego." He pulled the knife in a quick move, scalping the branch. The bark slid off the branch in one piece and flew halfway across the yard, and the knife flashed again, sending a sliver of greenwood aspen in the direction of the bark. "Two guys named Tom and their wives." Another sliver of aspen. "All of 'em are in IT, which don't stand for Idiot Training if you find yourselves tempted to ask."

The guests were sheathed in fleece and slippers. They followed Travis out of the bunkhouse, rubbing their eyes, and huddled in a half circle around Marvin, waiting for him to get up so they could go into the house.

Marvin didn't even look up. He sliced at the wood, and discarded aspen slivers piled on the porch steps. Finally one of the Toms mustered the courage to ask Marvin what he was making.

"Ain't making nothin'," Marvin said. "I'm whittling. If I was carving, that'd be a different story. Carving, you're making something; whittling, you're just passin' time."

"He's doing it again," one of the wives said to the other. "He's not being nice."

"At least there's cowboys today," the other wife replied.

"We're having a real-life cattle drive today," Travis said. "They're here to help."

Marvin swung his plaster cast off the porch. We all went inside and sat down at a table covered with platters of food—scrambled eggs and home-cured bacon, home-made biscuits, and hashed-brown home fries. The coffee was served in mismatched mugs, piping hot.

"Do you have kefir?" Bald Tom asked Rose.

Rose shook her head. "Don't even know what it is."

"How about a low-cholesterol egg substitute?"

"Nope," Rose said. "Just regular eggs."

Not-Bald Tom pointed at the home fries. "What are these fried in?"

"Same as everything else," Rose said.

"I'd like to send this back." Bald Tom held out his plate. "I want whole-grain pancakes instead."

"This is our kitchen," Marvin said, "not a goddamn restaurant. You'll eat what you're served, and by God, you'll like it."

We finished breakfast in silence. Afterward the guests

went back to the bunkhouse to change into their riding clothes while Rose cleaned up the kitchen. Marvin went back to his whittling. Slade and I followed Rick and Travis to the corral beside the barn. Travis chose our horses and helped us saddle them while Rick whistled for his own horse, a big sorrel gelding named Trouble. Travis let the stirrups on my saddle down a notch too far. When he glanced over my horse's withers, his jaw dropped.

We followed Travis's incredulous stare. The guests were picking their way across the pasture, looking like what I expected, jeans and jackets, all except for Not-Bald Tom, whose hands were poised for balance, wearing a brand-new Stetson that cast a long shadow across his face. He was decked out in cowboy clothes less real than those Slade and Rick were wearing. Not-Bald Cowboy Tom had brand-new Levi's, a brand-new shirt that looked inspired by the cover of a Garth Brooks album, brand-new Riata boots, and brand-new leather chaps. With fringe.

"Hey there, Tom." Rick gave Trouble's cinch one last tug and dusted his hands on his pants. "Duck on through that fence there and we'll get you saddled up." Cowboy Tom's chaps got hung up on the corral rails when he stuck a leg through the poles, and he decided to climb over the top. The other guests followed.

One of the wives touched my arm. "I'm Lynn," she said, "and this is Laura. What's your name?"

"Karol."

Lynn looked disappointed, and I couldn't figure out why.

"Karol Many Feathers," Slade said. Rick faked a cough to cover up a laugh, and Lynn looked a little more satisfied.

"Which reservation do you live on?" Laura asked.

"I live in Laramie," I said.

"I didn't know there was a reservation in Laramie," Lynn said.

"Tom and I even talked about moving there," Laura said. "Before we go home, let's take a look at Cody."

I just stared at the wives. Something unspoken passed between Travis and Rick and rippled across the corral until Slade and I were part of it, too.

"You ever rode?" Rick asked. The guests shook their heads.

"I hope I get a good horse," Laura said to Lynn. "A really pretty one."

Travis put her on Archie, a fat, bald-faced pinto with a lazy eye. Lynn's horse was a bay mare, just like the half-dozen other bay mares in the corral, and I could tell by her face that she wished she'd gotten a more special ride. Rick put Bald Tom on a half-Appaloosa gelding. Bald Tom's pant legs hitched up when he got his loafers settled in the stirrups, and despite his efforts to tug them down, both pant legs just hitched right back up the minute the horse took a step or two.

"That's gonna blister for sure," Rick said, as Bald Tom rode across the corral. "When he takes those socks off tonight, his skin's gonna be stuck to 'em from a day's worth of rubbing against leather and horse hair." He didn't sound vindictive or vengeful; it was just a statement of fact. Bald

Tom hadn't pissed off anyone but Marvin, but it wasn't Rick's fault that Bald Tom didn't have enough sense to wear boots when he rode.

Travis's eyes went from unsaddled horse to Cowboy Tom to the next unsaddled horse to Cowboy Tom until he'd contemplated every horse in the corral. He walked over to a huge black gelding on the far side of the corral and led the horse back to Cowboy Tom. "You'll be riding him," he said.

Rick leaned against the fence and pulled a piece of hay out of his mouth, pointing it at the gelding. "You ain't putting him on Widowmaker, are you?" he asked. A look of alarm settled on Cowboy Tom's face.

"Don't mind Rick," Travis said. "Widowmaker's a fine horse. We keep him around for fat kids from the city who ain't never rode. He's big and slow. The name's just a joke."

"If that's what you want to believe, fine by me." Rick shrugged.

Widowmaker stood like a statue while Travis swung a saddle onto him so gracefully that it might have dropped from the sky to land perfectly on the horse's back. Stirrups and cinch straps fell where they ought to, and the saddle was perfectly centered on the striped blanket beneath it. As Travis began to tighten the cinch, the horse heaved a deep, long breath, expanding his girth considerably. Travis pushed his knee behind the cinch strap and gave a quick, strong pull on the cinch, causing Widowmaker to exhale, deflate, and grunt in an aggrieved way. Travis looped the cinch strap around itself and pulled it tight. He stood back and looked at Cowboy Tom.

"Get on up, then, and we'll be on our way," Travis said, patting the seat of the saddle. Cowboy Tom reached uncertainly toward it. The horse swung its head around, looked Tom square in the eye, and snorted. Cowboy Tom hesitated.

"Okay," Travis said. "Let's start over. This ain't a machine. Walk around to his head and touch him. Let him smell you. Like this." Travis lifted the horse's head in both hands and scratched the big black cheeks. He stroked the nose and breathed softly into the horse's left nostril. The horse's eyelids dropped and he nickered softly.

"Now you," Travis said.

Cowboy Tom scratched the white blaze on the black forehead and blew toward the horse's nose. He trailed his fingers down between the horse's eyes and let them follow the basins between the nostrils and the cheekbones.

"Wow," he said. "It's like velvet. Incredible."

"Yep," Travis said. "Now go back around to the side there and take hold of the reins with your left hand. That's it. You always want to mount from the left. Grab that stirrup with your right hand and turn it out, toward the horse's shoulder." Cowboy Tom did as he was told, and looked at Travis for further instructions.

"Now you gotta put your foot in the stirrup," Travis said. "Take hold of the saddle horn, pull yourself up, and throw that other leg over."

Cowboy Tom looked surprised to find himself on top

of a horse. He grinned and gave the reins a tug and then he
flapped them a little bit. Widowmaker jerked his head up
and down.

"Don't yank on them reins," Travis said. "It just makes
him mad. All you got to do is touch the reins to the side of
his neck when you want him to turn. To get him started,
you just got to squeeze your legs and nudge him with your
heels." Cowboy Tom did as he was told, and Widowmaker
walked a few steps and stopped. "Do it again," Travis said.
"Harder this time. See if you can't work him up to a trot."

Widowmaker jogged around the corral, and Cowboy
Tom bounced up and down as though his head was going
to snap off.

"Loosen up on them reins," Travis said. He swung
gracefully into his horse's saddle and nodded at the guests.
Rick opened the gate and Travis rode out. Widowmaker
stepped into line behind Travis's horse, dropping his head

until his nose was six inches from the tail of Travis's horse. His head didn't move after that.

"Is he supposed to be doing this?" Cowboy Tom asked.

"He used to be a trail horse at a dude ranch," Travis called back. "You know, where one wrangler leads a bunch of folks real slow on a string of horses? They get like that and then they ain't good for anything else. Don't pay it any attention."

We rode across the yard, the only sounds the creaky squeak of saddles and the clatter of horses' hooves as we crossed the highway, the only pavement we'd see all day. Late August meant Indian summer, nights that were winter-cold and waking to the unexpected sight of your own breath and frost on the still-green grass. It's the kind of weather that catches most people unaware, the chill creeping through the night like a burglar and lingering past breakfast like an unwelcome houseguest.

The frost turned dewy and evaporated as soon as the sun crested over the hills, and the temperature rose rapidly until the feeling was back in my fingers. It smelled like summer then. Delicate wispy filaments of cirrus clouds converged on the horizon and a sage-scented breeze stirred dust and grasses. We rode until we were behind the herd, fanning the cattle into a line. The ranch dogs yipped wildly and nipped at the heels of wayward calves. Rick and Travis twirled lariats and yipped as loudly as the dogs.

The prairie extended to the horizon without being interrupted by a single building or blacktop road. Marvin's summer pasture was less than half a day's ride from his

winter pasture, a ride that didn't really count as a cattle
drive in the Old West sense of the term. The summer pasture was a highland basin, a wide swath of scrub brush and
sage. The rolling hills were freckled with gaunt, wind-
crippled pine trees and scarred outcroppings of the underlying granite.

By the time we got to the summer pasture, the guests
had had enough. They staggered off their horses and
grabbed the insides of their thighs, massaging muscles
stretched and burning from four hours in the saddle. Rose
had driven a truck up in a half hour or less and set up a bar-
becue grill, and was busy with beef when we got there.
Marvin was propped in a lawn chair in the bed of the truck,
and everything but the meat was lined up, buffet-style, on
the tailgate. The guests headed for the food like they hadn't
eaten in weeks, piling paper plates high with corn on the
cob, potato salad, Texas toast, and steak.

HALFWAY THROUGH his sirloin, Cowboy Tom asked Marvin where such a tasty steak might have come from. Marvin's eyes flickered across his herd. "You're kidding, right?"
he asked.

"Even our best butcher shop back home doesn't sell
anything like this," Cowboy Tom said. "I just want to know
where I can buy it."

"You know those cattle you looked at all morning?"
Marvin said. "Chances are you're eatin' one of them mama
cows' mamas."

Laura spit out the bite she'd just taken. "That's disgusting," she said.

"That's why I don't eat meat," I told her. "Feels a little hypocritical, don't you think?"

"Don't you have some folklore or something?" Lynn asked me.

"Excuse me?" I asked back.

"Yeah," Bald Tom said. "Don't you have some native stories or something?"

I'd forgotten the wig. I pulled the fake braids forward and smoothed my feathers. "Oh, sure," I said. "Anything in particular you were wanting?"

"Something sweet," Lynn said, taking another bite of Marvin's beef. "Something to remember."

"There's this story," I said, "about the buffalo. Where they went. You know how everything the Indians had came from the buffalo? Food and teepees, even their clothes. The Indians remembered to thank the buffalo for giving up their lives so that the Indians could live. But then the white men came, and they killed the buffalo for all the wrong reasons."

Marvin popped open another can of beer from the cooler beside him. Lynn and Laura seemed transfixed.

"One day," I went on, "when there weren't many buffalo left, they gathered by a mountain, and the side of the mountain opened up, like a door to another world. Everything inside was green and fresh and pure, like Wyoming was before the white men came, beautiful rivers, flowers, and fields of sweet grass. The buffalo went into this world and the mountain closed behind them. Some people say they live there still. They say you can hear them running, if you sit on the side of the mountain late at night when the moon is full and red."

"That's a beautiful story," Lynn said. "Did you make it up?"

"Of course not," I said.

Marvin chuckled the whole time. Afterwards, I climbed up into the bed of the truck and sat on the side. Slade leaned against the outside of the pickup bed, tossing my braids back and forth.

"It's been quite a day," Marvin said. "Thanks for coming up. Haven't laughed like this since the first guests came by."

"What happened to your leg?" I asked.

"Horse fell on me." Marvin opened another beer and watched as foam streamed down the sides of the can.

"Why?" Slade asked.

Marvin looked at him and gave him a halfway smile, crooking the corners of his mouth up on one side. "I ain't real sure," he said. "I think he wanted to impress the guests."

Chapter Eight

THE MAN WHO PIERCED my nipples looked like Santa Claus. He was short and round, with long white hair held back in a fluffy ponytail and a flyaway beard. His blue eyes crinkled above a smile that was more naughty than nice, but the chuckle he gave me as he shook my hand was a *ho, ho, ho,* no doubt about it, with the gruffness you'd expect once you learned Santa was a chain-smoker. His black Harley-Davidson T-shirt didn't diminish his jolly-old-elf likeness, and the tattoos that ran the length of his arms and crept up around his neck into his hairline just made him more like my kind of Santa.

Slade had introduced me to the idea of body piercing less than a year before. He subscribed to piercing magazines filled with body parts skewered, punctured, pierced, and stabbed in every way imaginable. He sought out pierced people and brought them to the tattoo shop with the triumphant glee of a cat dragging home a half-dead bird.

"Hey, take a look at this!" Slade grinned as he came into the tattoo shop, followed by a man I'd never seen before, a man who was unbuttoning his pants as he walked toward me. Slade nodded approvingly as the stranger dropped his jeans and held out a penis that appeared to be littered with scrap metal. A thick gold hoop curved out of the natural opening in the end and back through a pierced hole under the head, and the underside was polka-dotted with a dozen barbell studs.

"Hmm," I said. I wondered if the penis was even functional at this point, or if an erection would cause it to blow to bits.

In time, however, piercing came to seem as ordinary as tattooing, despite the impermanence of metal-punctured flesh and the speed with which most pierced skin knits itself back together, and I was thinking about having my nipples pierced. I liked how it looked, shiny slender hoops through delicate flesh.

Rick had an errand to run in Denver, and I asked if I could go along. He didn't look very happy about saying yes, and it wasn't until I'd spent thirty minutes waiting in his truck outside a strange house in a creepy neighborhood that I realized his reluctance might have had more to do with the nature of the errand than my company. We were headed back to Interstate 80 when I asked if we could

make a quick stop, like it was a whim, not something I'd
been planning for weeks. I gave him directions, one turn at
a time, until we got to Colfax Street and parked in front of
the Emporium of Design, a tattoo and piercing shop that
doubled as a retail outlet for clothing (mostly fetish) and
toys (all sex). I met Santa, explained what I wanted, picked
out my jewelry, and swore to come back in an hour, after
the 16-gauge stainless steel hoops had been autoclaved. We
went across the street, to the International House of Pancakes, and waited.

"Are you sure you want to do this?" Rick asked. "I
mean, if you want to, it's fine, and I'll go with you. I just
want you to be sure you want to."

"I want to," I said. "I've thought about it a lot."

"How much do you think it's going to hurt?" Rick
sipped his coffee.

I tried to picture it, and shuddered. "Maybe it's better
to not think about it."

After an hour, we went back. Santa led us into the
piercing room, which was a lot like a doctor's office, except
for the heavy-metal music. And the merchandise on racks
and mannequins. And all the tattoos.

"Have a seat." Santa pointed at a paper-covered exam
table, and I perched on the edge. Rick sat in a desk chair on
the other side of the room. He looked like someone who'd
been beamed in from a parallel universe and wanted desperately to go home. Santa patted my arm and gave me a
smile as he snapped on a pair of latex gloves.

"You can take off your shirt now," he said.

I realized, for the first time, that having my nipples pierced would involve exposing my breasts to a total stranger, and not the total stranger of my choosing. The door opened, and a young man and a woman came into the room.

"This is Greg," Santa said. "He'll be helping with the piercing. Donna will get you all set up."

Donna spent quite a while making dots with a pen and stretching a piece of dental floss between my nipples. She dotted, measured, wiped off the dots, measured, and dotted again.

Santa went for the right nipple first. Greg tweezed it in a pair of sterile clamps and Santa shoved a needle through, into a piece of cork. It happened quickly, in a blinding flash of agony. Waves of pain went coursing through my whole body. The biggest part of the pain hadn't even reached my brain before Santa started in on the left nipple. Greg clamped and Santa shoved, gritted his teeth, and shoved some more.

"Whatcha been doing with this one?" he asked.

"The exact same things she's been doing with the other one," Rick said.

Once the needle has pierced the skin, the jewelry is inserted into the hollow part of the end of the needle and lubricated, and the needle/jewelry assembly is worked through the hole. That's what they did, Santa and Greg and Donna. Donna gave me a mirror before Santa bandaged my nipples, and at that moment, it was all worth it. It was the first time I've looked at my own breasts and not compared them to someone else's, not wished that they were larger or smaller or rounder or higher.

My NIPPLES WERE almost healed two months later when Rick and I drove through Laramie late at night. He was meandering east with a purpose, past the hospital and golf course before turning onto a street that wove through Alta Vista, a neighborhood known for fancy houses, shrubbery mosaics, and meandering streets with conquistador names in alphabetical order. It's the kind of neighborhood where people were bound to notice when Rick took a corner on two wheels.

A few blocks farther, the asphalt had sunk on a curve near a fire hydrant, forming a dip ten feet wide and a foot deep at the curb, tapering into a shell-shaped depression as it edged into our lane. Rick swerved gracefully around the shallow end, smiled at me, and floored the accelerator. He fishtailed the truck in a U-turn, revved the motor, and slammed it into gear. The speedometer was quivering around sixty when we hit the dip, and Rick pulled the steering wheel hard toward the curb so the tires hit the dip at the deepest point.

It was like the first drop of a roller coaster. The truck sailed up the far side of the dip like a rocket lifting off, soaring into the air and bouncing on all four tires when it came down. I hadn't even caught my breath when I heard the siren behind us. Rick opened the glove box, took out a crumpled brown paper bag, and shoved it into the front of his pants.

"No sir, officer," Rick said, "didn't even see that dip. Hell of a surprise, I tell ya." He charmed his way from a ticket to a warning, polite and apologetic, and took a long time putting his license back in his wallet, watching in the rearview mirror as the police car drove away. He turned the key in the ignition, revved the motor twice, and grinned at me. He drove sedately for several blocks before he whipped the truck around and floored it, taking the dip even faster this time, driving down the wrong side of the street.

Rick pulled into a driveway, left the engine running, and turned up the volume on the tape deck. "Wait here," he said. He fumbled in his pants as he walked toward the door, palming the brown paper bag in one hand as he rang the bell. He returned a few minutes later, pushing a folded wad of money into his pocket. His face was pale under his tan, and he didn't look at me when he got into the truck.

"What happened?" I asked.

"I've been meaning to tell you something." Rick slammed his foot down hard on the accelerator and peeled away from the curb. He turned his head toward me and I caught a whiff of Jim Beam mingled with the sick-sweet smell of crack cocaine. His pinpoint pupils drilled into my eyes as he pulled onto the interstate, driving way faster than the posted speed limit on the hairpin on-ramp. The truck fishtailed once, but Rick pulled it straight. We passed every car in sight, my head pressed against the back of the seat from the force of the speed.

Rick yanked the steering wheel hard to the right, and

the car skidded across a gravel shoulder, into the guardrail, and I felt my door give a little. The fender sparked against the steel, and I screamed. Rick pulled the car away from the rail, sped up, and slammed into the guardrail again.

"Stop it. Just stop it!" I tried to keep the fear out of my voice, but I screamed again and grabbed at the steering wheel when he slammed into the rail a third time. "Stop the car. What are you doing?"

He looked at me, surprised, like he'd forgotten I was in the truck. "Sorry," he said. "I guess I just lost my head for a minute." He smiled, and the windshield reflected a ripple of us together, which was and was not a lie.

That's when he told me about the Navy recruiter. "I filled out all the papers, signed my name. Just gotta take a test or something, and it's done," he said. "I just don't know for sure that it's what I want."

"Why'd you do it then?" I asked. I couldn't imagine Rick taking orders from anyone, couldn't picture him in a uniform.

"I got fired," he said.

"How long ago?"

"A month. Maybe more."

"Why didn't you tell me?" I asked.

"Didn't want you to be disappointed."

I reached over and put my arms around him. I had to wait a good five minutes before he relaxed into my hug. "Do you need some money or anything?"

Rick let out a bitter chuckle. "Nope. Doing fine for

money, but it's one thing to sell a gram or two on the side, and it's something altogether different to make a living like this. I don't have any choices left. Even if I felt like getting too old too fast and being cold all the time, Pop's selling the ranch, so there's no cowboying to do. Probably a good thing anyway, being as how cattle hate me almost as much as I hate them. And now all the body shops in town want someone with a Wyo Tech diploma, not some-body like me, so if the Navy don't take me, I might as well be dead."

"Anything at all I can do?"

"Well, I could use a tattoo." Rick smiled.

"Okay," I said. "Come by the shop first thing tomorrow—"

"I could sort of really use a tattoo right now."

"It's almost midnight," I said. I didn't say anything about crack or Jim Beam.

"I know it's late," Rick said, "but it would make me feel better. Please?"

I nodded and kissed him. A few minutes later, I un-locked the door to the shop and flicked on the lights. "You know what you want?"

"Something of yours. You can pick."

I'd been drawing retro-style pinup girls for months, keeping the exaggerations I thought made them kitschy and cool, but without the crossed eyes I kept seeing on flash sheets. I drew big hips and big breasts, but I also drew fingers with nails and features that were proportional to their faces. I wanted to see if it would work on skin, if I could tattoo a pinup girl who would look old-fashioned but feel brand-new. I grabbed my sketchbook and flipped through it until I found what I was looking for. The pinup girl was wearing red stiletto heels and nothing else. One finger was hooked into her pouty mouth, and she had an angel's halo above her coiffed curls and a devil's tail curling around her legs.

I held out the sketch pad so Rick could see. "Would you let me tattoo this?" I asked. "On your arm?"

"She's so cool," Rick said, touching the paper hesitantly. "Is she old?"

"No. She's new. It's just the old style."

I used a five-needle outliner instead of the tight three I normally used, and left uncolored skin inside the outline, off-line shading, just like in the pictures I'd seen of pinup-girl tattoos from the 1940s. Vivid red with purple shading for the devil's tail and shoes, gold and orange for the hair. I photographed the tattoo before I bandaged Rick's arm and cleaned up the shop after he went home.

The next morning, I got up late, went to work late, and told Slade what had happened.

"Rick's joining the Navy?" Slade laughed. "What was he thinking?"

"Same thing he's always thinking, I guess," I said. We looked at each other for a long minute and then broke eye contact. Otherwise we'd have to talk about Rick's thinking, and Slade wouldn't be laughing anymore. Slade shook his head and I stared down at the palms of my hands. "Can I have a few days off?" I asked.

"As many as you need." Slade hugged me.

Ⓐ WEEK OR SO LATER, I woke up one morning, tangled in my pillow and two of Rick's *Mopar Action* magazines, and looked over at Rick—leaned over, actually—to take a good, long look at his face. I was hit with a cloud of half-digested Jim Beam. I moved his arm and found a set of ratchet heads pocking his skin, stuck to his arm. The sheets smelled, Rick smelled, and once I managed to muster the courage to face the truth, I realized that I smelled, too.

When I got out of bed, I noticed the *Hustler* magazine Rick had clasped in one hand, the other hand dangling off the bed into a pile of dirty underwear tucked into a rusting tire rim. Again.

I showered and put on a pretty dress and went straight to work. Slade smiled big when he saw me, and offered me half of his day's appointments. It was the beginning of the week of Jubilee Days, and Laramie was swollen with tourists, many of whom wanted to go home with a tattoo souvenir.

The downtown streets were cordoned off in a three-block T. Picnic tables were arranged around food vendors; tourists and locals and cowboys milled about, eating Navajo tacos and barbecued shredded beef on white-bread buns. The open-container ordinance had been lifted, and watery, foamy beer was sold in plastic cups from kegs in the backs of pickup trucks.

From inside the shop we had a ringside seat for the

festivities, which seemed to have become more farcical and less western with each year that passed.

A flatbed truck served as a makeshift stage for melo- dramas and western skits. Someone from the Jubilee Days Committee told Slade to turn down the music, a *Faith No More* album with the volume loud enough to shake the walls of the shop. A dozen women wearing neon-colored sport-bras and matching shorts arranged low plastic benches in a semicircle and performed thirty minutes of step aero- bics in sync with dance music on a tape player hooked up to the PA system.

The men in the audience seemed to enjoy the aerobics more than the skits. They hooted and whistled and cheered. The women studiously stepped onto the benches and jumped back down, clapping in time with the music. A few of them were lip-syncing the lyrics to the songs, and a few others moved their lips in a one-two-three-clap count.

We were almost done for the day when two men came into the shop. I couldn't tell if they were cowboys or tourists; they were wearing brand-new western clothes, like the tourists usually did, but they seemed more at home in their outfits.

"Can I help you?" I asked.

"I'm Justin, and this is Chris," the taller one said. "We want to get tattoos."

"We *need* to get tattoos," Chris corrected him. "I need one desperately because I'm wallowing in an abyss of exis- tential despair, but Justin just likes to collect consumerized rebellion."

"I hear that any would-be rebel with fifty bucks can buy into the illusion that a tattoo will make him cool," Justin said. "Is that true?"

"He needs a tattoo to go with his stone-washed jeans and his ponytail," Chris said.

"Are you for real?" I asked.

Justin and Chris fell against each other, laughing. "No," Justin said. "We just wanted to have some fun. We do want tattoos, though."

"Cool," I said. Slade came out of the back, and, since they didn't care which one of us did whose tattoo, we agreed to do one each. Before we even got started, Justin and Chris spent enough time talking that we knew they were from Chicago, that they were both software consultants, that they had been a couple for more than a decade. They wanted matching tattoos, red hearts and banners— "master" in Chris's banner and "slave" in Justin's, even though they said that part was mostly a joke—on their left buttocks.

Chris and Justin hugged us both, tipped us big, and announced that they were going to go shopping. When Rick showed up around closing time, we locked the doors and went outside to watch the first-ever Jubilee Days cattle drive.

I would like to think that I am not the only person who envisioned a cattle drive just like the ones in the movies. I expected mayhem—crazy-eyed steers rocketing from one end of town to the other, out of control, pursued by cowboys perched atop galloping horses, frothy with sweat.

Instead, two police cars, side by side, inched along at a parade pace, lights flashing deceptively quickly and portending a reverent excitement. The police cars were followed by a child-sized covered wagon that was pulled by two Shetland ponies, driven by a beer-gutted man in a plaid cowboy shirt and straw hat who waved pleasantly at the crowd as he urged the straining ponies onward. His knees were tucked almost to his chin so that his feet wouldn't drag on the ground. Plaid-covered belly flab oozed over both sides where his thighs met his stomach. His height and his girth exaggerated the diminutive dimensions of both the wagon and his team. A banner draped over the canvas-covered wagon back advertised Northridge Discount Liquors in big red letters.

The Rodeo Queen and her attendants followed the covered wagon. They rode sleek, well-groomed quarter horses that danced down the street. The women were a symphony of pastels, from their color-coordinated hats to their matching boots, with banners pinned across their ample bosoms announcing their Rodeo-royalty titles. The queen was resplendent in hues of purple, from the brushed-felt violet of her hat to the lavender denim of her jeans to the opalescent snaps on the cuffs of her blouse. Her boots, also purple, matched her horse's hackamore and saddle blanket.

Behind the Rodeo royalty, the forty-five steers were lumped together in one big, slow, shaggy mound. Nine across, five deep. Shoulder to shoulder, nose to tail. The steers were small docile creatures who were guided in tight

formation by an entourage of cowboys on horseback. The
animals were oblivious to the crowd they'd drawn. They
plodded along, heads down and hooves clacking against
the asphalt, as though they knew: *This year, the fairgrounds;
next year, the slaughterhouse.* The first step toward their rodeo
limelight and hamburger destiny was a two-mile walk on
July pavement. You couldn't help feeling sorry for them.

Two more police cars, lights flashing, trailed behind
the cattle, and a pair of street sweepers brought up the rear.
The sounds of steel brushes and bursts of water and vacu-
ums drowned out the sounds of the cattle.

After the cattle drive we just hung around, watching
the tourists watching us: Rick, all shirtless and slouchy;

Slade, in a better mood than usual for Jubilee Days; and me in a summer dress.

"Excuse me." A woman tapped Rick's shoulder. "Could you move over? You're blocking my shot. I want a picture of the cowboys."

We moved over and looked in the direction of her camera lens. The shutter snapped merrily, capturing image after image of Justin and Chris, complete with spurs and chaps. They looked like they'd stepped off the cover of a Top-40 country album. Rick shook his head and Slade laughed out loud.

"Do you think she'll notice that they're holding hands when she gets her pictures back?" Slade asked. "And if she does notice, do you think she'll think that it's just another manly western custom?"

Rick's GOING-AWAY party started, as most parties did, in the back room of Slade's tattoo shop. I parked in the lot near the train depot, next to a 1972 Roadrunner that had been parked in the same space for months, collecting dust and bird droppings while its dashboard curled in the sun. Laramie isn't like a big city; a person could leave a car most anyplace for months and find it intact, save for the ravages of weather, but even in the half-light of dusk, something was definitely not quite right with the Roadrunner. I walked around the car twice. Three of the tires were gone—rims, too—and the axles were propped on blocks of wood.

And just three wheels were missing. Seemed to me a person would want to take an even number.

When I got to the shop, Rick was already there, sprawled in the tattoo chair with his arms crossed behind his neck, tufts of armpit hair peeking out from the place where sleeves were once attached to his T-shirt. My eyes wandered across the shapes of his biceps, mentally tracing my way from one tattoo to another, down to his wrists, his huge hands, his knobby fingers, his grease-caked nails. I had a sneaking suspicion about the Roadrunner.

"Why didn't you take all four?" I wasn't blaming him, necessarily. Just curious.

Rick shrugged. "Couldn't get the lug nuts off." Like so many of his explanations, it wasn't a question of right or wrong, it was simply a matter of lug nuts.

Rick and I had agreed that breaking up before he shipped out would eliminate some inevitable heartbreak, especially since he said that he was never, ever, coming back to Wyoming, and I didn't want to live anyplace else. Slade was hosting the dissolution of our relationship. Even though I thought I should be sad, Slade's enthusiasm was contagious. Rick slid over to make room for me in the tattoo chair. We kissed and shrugged and laughed while Slade spooned half a can of orange juice into a blender, along with a cup of water and a foul-smelling handful of dried mushrooms. The resulting concoction was a chunky, nasty-tasting cocktail, and we toasted each other and the U.S. Navy with paper cups and tried to gulp it down without gagging, swallowing burps and dry heaves.

Slade had an idea, and we all agreed it was a good one. Rick washed his hands while Slade got out a tattoo machine and I carefully traced the words from a book of fancy lettering. We laughed as the tracing went through the thermofax, laughed even more when the stencil was on the side of Rick's hand.

"Are you sure this is the one you're supposed to salute with?" I asked.

"Rick is about to become a member of the finest armed forces in the world," Slade said. "He's about to risk his life at sea to protect our constitution and freedom and shit. I'm sure he knows which hand you use for a salute."

"Can't be sure," Rick said. "Haven't had to do it yet."

Fifteen minutes later the tattoo was done, and tears were streaming down Slade's cheeks, he'd been laughing so much. Rick stood up and saluted himself in the mirror. Even from across the room, "fuck off" was more than legible; it was impossible to ignore.

The next thing I knew, it was past midnight, and Slade and Rick and I were in Slade's Chevelle convertible, careening up a hill on the Lincoln highway. We piled out of the car in a parking lot in Vedauwoo, a sprawling rock formation east of Laramie. Slade had stopped at the liquor store before our little trip, and he handed me two plastic bags, a six-pack of long-neck Budweisers in each. I held my arms out for balance and took three steps before tripping over a concrete parking block. This mishap resulted in four broken bottles and a shower of foam, but no one seemed to mind. Rick laughed from far away while Slade rearranged the remaining bottles, an equal number in each bag. We spent a very long time picking up broken glass and depositing it in the backseat of the Chevelle.

I followed Slade and Rick over the rocks. There was a path someplace, but we couldn't find it. Rick reached back and took my hand from time to time, helping me over the rough spots. We found the secret passage and dropped to our knees. I thought another beer bottle had broken, but I couldn't be sure.

We crawled through a tunnel of broken boulders, emerging in a small amphitheater on a precipice with a hundred-foot drop, straight down, to a soft green meadow. I'd forgotten that this was where we were going, so I was pleasantly surprised.

Rick took a beer from one of the bags and opened it. He stood on the very edge, causing an avalanche of pebbles with his feet. He rocked back and forth, unsteady, and I wished that he would step back and sit down. Slade stood beside Rick and watched solemnly as Rick flicked the cap from his beer bottle into the air. It tinkled and plinked forever.

I lurched to my feet and walked unsteadily to the edge of the rocks. Looking down made me dizzy. Slade put his hand on my arm.

"It's a long way down," I said.

"It's nice," Rick said. He was no longer wearing a shirt. It was in his hand, waving in the breeze like a flag over the precipice. In slow motion, Rick's hand opened and the shirt swirled like a leaf. A bird's wing. Down and out and floating up. Then it was gone.

"One step, man," Rick said. "You ever think about it? One step and it's all over."

We thought about this for a minute and tried to see where the shirt had landed.

"When you're faced with death," Slade said, "you learn the truth about life. And the truth is this. What you want most is not to save your soul, assuming that you have one, but to live. In your body. Flesh is truth."

Rick snapped to attention and saluted with a flourish. "Aye, aye, sir." A little blood had dripped down the side of Rick's hand, had crusted in places on his new tattoo, but the words were still clearly visible. The three of us sat down and dangled our feet in the air beneath the rocks, drinking beer in silence and watching the sun come up. Slade leaned against my shoulder and I leaned against Rick, face to face with the pinup girl I'd tattooed. I watched her hips wiggle on Rick's arm. For a moment I pretended that I was her, two-dimensional breasts pulsing with the warmth of a man's flesh, a possession, bought and paid for. Red lips pursed in perpetual surprise, brows arched over a come-fuck-me stare. It would be nice, I thought, to be a two-dimensional woman sometimes, nothing to do but point my inky fingers at three-dimensional people.

Chapter Nine

TATTOO ARTISTS VACATION differently than most people; we figure out where we'd like to go, then start calling shops to see if anyone would be interested in having a guest artist for a while. Slade had gone to San Diego for a two-week working vacation at a place called Avalon, but when he got there, business was slow. He worked one day; that was it. But everyone felt bad and started calling other artists in other shops, and Slade wound up spending his vacation at Ace Tattoo, working for an artist named Steve Smith. Steve and Slade, it turned out, had known each other indirectly for years. They became friends instantly, and, for most of 1991, Slade bounced back and forth between the Body Art Workshop in Laramie and Ace Tattoo in San Diego. A week here, a few weeks there.

Working in the tattoo shop wasn't much fun when Slade was out of town. I missed his jokes and I missed having someone besides the customers to talk to. Tattooing was the only job I'd ever had where I made a living as an artist, and for that, I loved it. It was stable, it had direction, and it was lucrative. As with any other job, I had to get up, get dressed, go to the shop, and work. And as with any other job, sometimes I just didn't want to do it. Sure, I didn't have to be there until noon, I could dress any way I chose, and between tattoos I could lie on the couch doing nothing, but it was still a job, especially when Slade was out of town.

I spent my days tattooing and my nights alone. Rick had gone up to the ranch to pack up some things, study for the Navy's entrance exams, and wait for his ship to come in, or whatever. Slade was gone, Rick was gone, and the loneliness echoed in my heart.

MICHELLE WAS a big girl, the kind of big that's on the far side of Rubenesque by even the most charitable stretch of both imagination and euphemism. She was shy and self-conscious when she came into the shop, crossing and un-crossing her arms as though apologizing for taking up so much space. She was just planning ahead, she said, wanted to get a tattoo someday, after she lost enough weight.

"Okay," I said. "Whenever you're ready. But if you want a tattoo, you can get one anytime. How much a person weighs doesn't matter. Tattoos go on the outsides of people."

"Really?" Michelle looked like this was the first and only time she'd heard "doesn't matter" in the same sentence as her weight. She sat down on the couch and started talking about how being fat had kept her from doing most everything else, how she wanted a tattoo more than ever and right now. She'd been overweight her whole life, criticized by her (thin) relatives, teased by classmates all the way through college, ignored by boys and invisible to men. She'd been thinking about her tattoo longer and more seriously than she let on at first. She blushed and grinned when I asked her what and where.

Fifteen minutes later, Michelle was sitting in the tattoo chair with a towel wrapped around her naked torso, and I was drawing on her with a felt-tip marker. A lifetime of self-conscious embarrassment had kept her out of tanning salons and swimming pools, and she wore clothing that covered as much as possible all year long, which meant that her skin was translucent and soft, more taut than skinny people's skin, a dream canvas. Michelle wanted hummingbirds, as many as it took, from the bottom of her shoulder blade, up and over her clavicle, down the side of her breast.

There was no black ink at all in Michelle's tattoo, no discernible outline. Each hummingbird was a different part of an Impressionist spectrum, and they were beautiful, hues of blue and green, red and orange, vivid against her pale skin.

Michelle's tattoo took several hours. I was almost done when the front door slammed open into the wall and two young men strode up to the tattoo-room window. "Hey, it's a *chick*," one of them said. I thought he might have meant to whisper. The second one pulled up his sleeve and stuck his arm into the tattoo room, right between me and Michelle.

"Got this back home a couple weeks ago," he said.

"It's not healing very well," I pointed out. The tattoo was a tribal band, riddled with holidays where it hadn't been solidly colored, with an outline that hung in tattered scabs.

"How much to color it in again?"

"A hundred dollars and at least two hours," I said.

He made a huffy sound in the back of his throat, "But the guy that did it only charged me fifty."

"Maybe he would have charged you more if he'd filled it in solid." I leaned under his arm and got back to the white highlights on the hummingbirds. "I wouldn't worry about having it redone for a while. You've got to let that skin heal completely before you can tattoo it again, and you're a long way from healed. What are you putting on it? Neosporin?"

"Preparation H," he said.

Michelle giggled.

"You might want to switch to Neosporin," I suggested, "or lotion."

He made the huffy sound again. "But the guy that did it told me to use Preparation H."

"Maybe he just thought you were an asshole," Michelle said.

I'd just finished cleaning up after Michelle's tattoo when my 4:30 appointment came in. I said hello, and she said, "We're going to have to smudge the place."

"What?" I asked. From the moment she opened the

door, Tiffany made it plain that this would be no ordinary tattoo appointment. It started with the two friends she brought along and the suitcase they hauled in. The friends, Darla and Sandy, were wearing layers of brightly patterned cotton clothing, dresses over skirts over roomy pants. Like Tiffany, their arms were armored from wrist to elbow with bracelets, and all three smelled as though they'd been marinated in a blend of patchouli, marijuana, and Oil of Olay.

"We're going to have to smudge the place," she repeated.

"Purify it," Darla said.

"It's a sterile environment," I said. "It's already pure."

"Not spiritually," Sandy said.

"How do you know?" I was genuinely curious.

"It could be," Darla amended, "but we have to be sure." She opened the suitcase and took out a hank of sagebrush that had been wrapped with a bright red string, lit the end of it, and waved the sage smoke into the corners of the waiting room.

My eyes were watering from the smoke as I asked Tiffany for her owl picture. It was a line drawing that needed a few minor corrections to work as a tattoo, and I started toward the tattoo room to redraw and stencil it.

"Just a minute," Sandy said. "We're not connected yet."

"We have to join hands, form a circle, and breathe together," Darla said.

"Go right ahead," I said. "It'll just take a few minutes to stencil Tiffany's design."

"No," Sandy said. "You have to connect with us."

"We have to have four," Darla added. "For the four directions. I'm North, Sandy's South, and Tiffany is East. Without you, there's no West."

"I'm about two seconds from throwing all three of you out of here," I said. "This is not the way I tattoo. Have you ever been to a tattoo shop before?"

All three shook their heads.

"But it's a tattoo of my totem animal," Tiffany said softly. "My totem animal found me on my very first vision quest, and I want my tattoo to be sacred."

"It can be as sacred as you want," I said. "But no more burning sagebrush, If you need to hold hands and connect or whatever, you can do it out here while I draw up the tattoo." I walked away without waiting for an answer. From the tattoo room, I could hear some quiet chanting and bracelets jingling impatiently.

"What?" Darla's indignant voice was loud enough to startle my pencil across the paper.

"It is, too, my totem animal," Tiffany said petulantly.

"Not if you saw the rabbit first," Sandy said.

"How many times do I have to tell you? The owl was there first, but she was in a tree, so I didn't notice her until she flew away. The rabbit was, like, following me, but the owl was really there first, even if I saw it second."

"Even if it was there first, you didn't see it first, so it can't be your totem animal," Darla said.

"Yeah," Sandy said. "The rabbit is your totem animal."

"It is *not*," Tiffany yelled. "I don't have rabbit traits—I have owl traits. The owl stands for awareness and intuition and courage. The owl is the totem animal for clairvoyants, right? The owl is about having the courage to follow your instincts."

"Yeah?" Darla yelled back. "So? It's still not your totem animal if you saw the rabbit *first.*"

"My instincts and my extrasensory abilities tell me that the owl is, too, my totem animal," Tiffany said. "Would a rabbit know that?"

"I'm ready to get started," I said, holding up the drawing for Tiffany's inspection.

"It's perfect." She handed it back and reached for the suitcase. "I'll be good to go as soon as I get my altar set up."

"No altar," I said.

"Incense?" Sandy asked.

"No."

Thirty minutes later, I was halfway through the tattoo when Tiffany sighed and said, "I am so glad that I'm finally having a rite of passage. I felt so left out before."

"Left out?" I asked.

"Yeah," Tiffany nodded emphatically. "Sandy and Darla already have their first tattoos. So does almost everybody I know."

"Do you know what 'hubris' is?" I asked. I wasn't going to start, I really wasn't. But I knew what Slade would have said, and I could be a little bit nicer about it than he would have been. And it really needed saying.

"Yeah," Darla said. "I made some last night. You take chickpeas and garlic and tahini and lemon—"

"That's hummus," Tiffany interrupted. "Hubris is something else. It's not a food."

"It's what happens when you combine arrogance and presumption," I said. "It's what you're doing right now. Tattooing is not a rite of passage in this culture, not even in your version of this culture. If it were, tattooing would be done by pastors and priests, and tattoos would be doled out when a person was ready, administered like sacraments when a person earned them."

"It *can* be a rite of passage, though," Sandy said. "My first tattoo was. The design really came from the deepest part of myself, and I got it when I was in a really important place in terms of my personal growth."

"It's an Americanized version of something that was important to people in other places," I said. "Your rite of passage is Americanly convenient. There's no tiresome waiting around for the shaman of your tribe to decide whether or not you've earned it. There's no one dragging you, kicking and screaming, out of your hut because it's time to commemorate the first day of your first-ever menstrual cycle with a tattooed mark. You get to decide whether or not a particular event qualifies as a rite of passage, and you get to decide what part of your body you'll tattoo to celebrate this event, the event that you chose. You get to choose the image that best suits this event, and it can be anything you want. You're not stuck with a charcoal-colored arrangement of geometric shapes and lines that would let everyone in the tribe know, right away, even if they were out hunting mammoths when your rite of passage took place, that you are a woman now."

I wiped the excess ink away from Tiffany's tattoo. The owl was almost finished, just the yellow and the white highlights left. "That's what I mean by hubris. As long as you haven't maxed out your Visa card, you can have a rite of passage whenever you want, and you can drag me into it by making me some kind of on-demand shaman without warning me ahead of time."

"Paying for it doesn't mean it isn't a rite of passage," Darla said. "You have to pay for it because that's how everything is now."

I ran the needles in the rinse cup and wiped them on the paper towel, dipped them in the white pigment, and finished up the highlights as quickly as possible.

The girls were packing their sage and whatnot into the suitcase when Rick's brother, Travis, came into the shop.

"Got something to tell you." Travis leaned his head through the window into the tattoo room. He looked like he hadn't slept in a few days.

"Okay," I said.

"Can we go someplace and talk?"

"Talk to me here," I said. I was scrubbing my tubes and in a hurry to go home.

Travis came around the corner, sat on the edge of the dentist's chair, got up, and sat on my stool. He got up again and just sort of paced around, even though the tattoo booth was too small to really accommodate that sort of thing.

"Navy turned Rick down," Travis said. "There was tests, and he flunked."

"Is he going to stay here then?" I was secretly happy; if he flunked, maybe he wouldn't leave, and then everything would go back to being the way it had been.

"I guess you could say that," Travis said. "I guess he's not going anywhere ever again. Rick's dead."

The tube I'd been scrubbing fell out of my hand. I heard it hit the counter, roll, and hit the floor, but the sounds were coming from very far away. "No he's not," I said. It could not possibly be true.

"Funeral's tomorrow. Pop would like it if you came. We all would."

"He can't be dead," I said. "There must have been a mistake."

"Only mistake was Rick getting Jim Beam and Jesus mixed up like he always does," Travis said. "Only mistake was him taking the high beams on an Oklahoma Peterbilt for the white light at the end of the tunnel. Or maybe there ain't no mistake at all, being as how he crossed three lanes of traffic and a borrow pit getting there."

I closed my eyes and saw the pinup-girl tattoo on Rick's arm instead of Rick's face, which is what I'd expected to see. I pictured her sightless eyes staring through the satin-lined darkness of a coffin somewhere.

The funeral was to be on the ranch, in the family cemetery near the original homestead cabin. Travis drew me a map and rattled off directions that consisted of vague references to local landmarks. "When you get to the fork by the old Hansen place, you're going to want to take a left. Road gets a little choppy. A few miles up, you'll come to the big stump trail, ain't nothing more than a pair of ruts marked by a big ol' lodgepole stump. Trail drops down into a valley south of the main Utopia shaft—'course you can't see it on account of it's all boarded up and overgrown, so never mind that part."

Travis shifted his weight and studied the map he was drawing. "Anyway, you'll come to this old tie hack camp, but don't follow the trail down in there. This time of year, the road turns to gumbo, and you'll never get back up the hill. So what you'll want to do is whip around here, kind of like so." He pressed the ballpoint pen into the paper to emphasize the route. "Go past the tailings, and follow the road through the trees. About half a mile more, the road hits the river in a shallow spot. Just drive on across and turn south when you get to the other side. Road picks up again when you're out of the rocks, and you'll come to a miner's cabin that burnt down about twenty years ago." Travis made a big X on the far side of the squiggly line of the river.

"Belonged to some guy who had a run of real bad luck after he got burnt out. Carved himself a cave in the side of the mountain and kept working his claim, and he went crazy real slow. Tried to end it all with a bullet, lost his nerve a little too late. He crawled down to the river and died from exposure. My granddad was the one who found him. Said he had a nasty little bullet furrow down the side of his head, but the blood had mostly clotted by the time he died." Travis paused and looked at me. "I used to always wonder whether he panicked or whether he just gave up. Freezing to death like that's a mighty slow way to go."

I nodded and tried to pick out the details that would make the difference between attending a funeral for someone I still couldn't believe was dead and getting lost.

"Anyhow," Travis went on, "past the burnt cabin you'll find a stand of trees, and past that, the prettiest meadow you ever seen, and past *that*, Cemetery Bluff. That's just what we call it, though, ain't like there's a sign hangin' on it."

After Travis left, I locked the door and curled up on the floor and sobbed. When I ran out of tears, I punched the linoleum until my hands ached. I got out my camera bag and opened the back of the Nikon, ruining the undeveloped, exposed film of Rick's pinup-girl tattoo. I told myself that I did it for truth-in-advertising reasons; putting the pictures in my portfolio implied that the tattoo was on the skin of someone still alive. The truth was that I wanted to keep the memory of that particular tattoo all to myself.

I couldn't sleep. Finally, around four in the morning, I gave up trying, got into my car, and drove toward the ranch.

I made it as far as the river in my car. The crossing was shallow only to someone in a four-wheel-drive truck or on horseback, so I left my car in the middle of the trail, took off my shoes and socks, breathed deeply, and stepped into the icy water, going as fast as I could without falling, feeling for sandy places between slippery rocks with my toes. I was numb to the ankles by the time I reached the other side of the river.

The burnt-out cabin was right where Travis said it would be, a crumbling chimney rising from charcoal logs. The trail led to what would have been the front door and veered off toward the meadow. A Sears Roebuck mail-order catalog, surprisingly well preserved, was half buried under a pile of brown pine needles. Rusty tin cans were everywhere, most of them unopened, all without labels, except for a can of creamed corn that had rolled under what was left of the porch. Part of the door frame still stood, charred and leaning dangerously. I stepped through and touched the dirty white stove that sat in the ashes like an enameled mushroom. The table was upside down; a person had to have done that, someone hard of heart who'd see an unlocked door as an invitation to pillage. I tipped the table right-side-up and smoothed the peeling red oilcloth tacked to the surface as best I could before sliding the table across the soft rot of the floor planks to the place it would have belonged had this been my own kitchen. No matter how I turned it, the table wobbled on uneven legs, and it sloped in more than one direction at a time.

I stooped beneath the warp of the door frame and looked back at the cabin. The burnt rubble was sad beneath the mammoth sculpture of the wind-smoothed granite mountainside that rose above the gnarled trees behind the ruined building. At the corner of the debris, I noticed a glass jar upended on a post; the metal lid was affixed to the

wood with a rusted spike, and the jar was screwed into the base. Inside the jar was a yellow piece of paper, folded.

I unscrewed the jar from its base. My fingers closed around the brittle paper, and I drew it carefully from the mouth of the jar. It fell apart as I unfolded it. I laid the four pieces on my palms, pieces as fragile as butterfly wings. The paper was an old placer claim, smudgy ink on government form lines, entitling Peter Svensen to mine for the riches of a particular piece of land.

I tried to reconcile the hope implied by the spidery handwriting on the claim with the disappointments implicit in the charred logs and debris strewn around my feet. I looked at the paper in my hands and thought about the story Travis had told. I put my own face on a crazy miner and imagined crawling, mad and bloody, down to the river to die in the snow.

The remnants of the placer claim blew into the weeds. The willow leaves gossiped in a low whisper down by the river. The wind picked up, and by the time it reached my face it was like tickling fingers, first from one direction and then from another. It made me think of Rick.

When I got to the bluff, Rick's horse, Trouble, was ground-tied and grazing behind Marvin's truck; the saddle was Travis's, the bridle looked brand-new, and sunlight gave a red-gold glow to the horse's freshly groomed coat. The bluff and the meadow belonged to Marvin, but since he was selling this part of the ranch, too, Rick wouldn't be buried with the others; they'd had him cremated. I tried not to think about this as I hiked up the side of the bluff, but when I saw the urn sitting in the shade under a tree, the pinup-girl tattoo crossed my mind again.

Nobody said much of anything for a long time. It was just me and Travis and Marvin; Rose was in the truck. She'd taken one of the pills her doctor had prescribed for the pain of her grief and fallen fast asleep. Marvin picked up the urn, put it back down, lurched across the bluff on his crutches to a tree, and stood with his back to us. "Might as well go ahead and do it," Marvin called. "Ain't got the stomach for it myself."

Travis gave the lid a little twist. "Wish you hadn't done it, Bro," he mumbled. "Selfish motherfucker. I'm gonna miss you." He finally got the lid off, looked inside, and looked up at the clouds. "You ever scatter someone before?" he asked.

I shook my head.

"Me either. You want to go first?"

A gust of wind came up as I tipped the urn sideways, catching bits of ash and pieces of things I didn't want to think about and whipping them away, mostly, except for a few pieces that flew up into Travis's face and my own. Travis spit.

"Sorry, Bro," he said. He took the urn and shook out the rest of what was left of Rick, and we stood carefully upwind, watching the ashes blow away. Travis screwed the lid back onto the urn and squinted in the direction the wind was blowing.

"Well," he said, "Rick always did want to travel."

Marvin was still standing with his back to us, leaning on the tree, his shoulders hunched under an ill-fitting black suit. I walked over and rubbed his arm, mostly because I didn't know what to say. Marvin took both my hands and held them, hiding my fingers with his big rough rancher hands. He stood there, staring down, for the longest time. Then he squinted up at the sky.

"It's a nice day, ain't it," he said. "A real fine day." And we all pretended that there wasn't a tear rolling down the side of his sunburned nose. We stood there for a long time, pretending up a storm. Marvin wasn't crying, Rick wasn't dead, and we were all standing around on that beautiful bluff just to admire the weather.

Chapter Ten

I COULD REMEMBER when Folger's coffee tasted just fine. By 1992, Folger's wouldn't do, not by a long shot.

What the people who moved here from other places wanted most, it seemed, was coffee and a place to drink it, and not just regular coffee, the kind you could get at the CK Chuckwagon or Rose Café, a bottomless mug of a bitter red blend. They wanted espresso blends and plastic bears filled with honey in case they couldn't decide between the white sugar, the raw sugar, and the artificial sweetener. They wanted atmosphere.

When the first coffeehouse opened, I went in, mostly because I wanted to know what a three-dollar cup of coffee tasted like. The menu was a confusing mélange of foreign words and dollar signs, above a rack of syrup bottles with flavors that looked like they belonged on a Sno-Kone cart. I didn't know the difference between a latte and a cappuccino, there was no explanation of Caffè Americano, and the cups came in tall, large, and grande. No medium, unless maybe large was medium and grande was large. When it was my turn, I ordered a latte, mostly because that's what the woman ahead of me had gotten.

"What size?" the waitress asked.

"Grand."

"That's grand-ay." She spent a lot of time knocking grounds out of something that looked like an ice-cream scoop, filling the scoop with ground coffee, and attaching it to a big machine. After it hissed and dripped for a while, she poured hot foamy milk and two shot glasses of espresso into the kind of tall glass that fancy restaurants serve beer in. I wanted to point out the reasons for having handles on cups that were filled with hot beverages, but I wrapped my glass in a handful of napkins and carried it to a quaint little table. I nibbled on a dried-out, turd-shaped cookie—biscotti, it was called. The cookie wasn't worth the saliva it took to soften it, so I wrapped it in my napkin and waited for the coffee to cool. I stuck my tongue in the milk foam on the top, and it didn't taste like anything.

THE WIND SWIRLED through downtown Laramie, tossing litter and leaves into doorways. Fluff from the cottonwood trees collected in the gutters. A summer thunderstorm pushed down low, streetlights refracted through dark clouds.

It was only eight o'clock, and the shop was supposed to stay open until nine, but I'd done plenty of business and the downtown was deserted.

As I turned the sign from OPEN to CLOSED, a man's face appeared in the doorway, menacing eyes above a full beard. I gasped. I was half in and half out, one hand on the closed sign and the other on the doorjamb. He reached his arm over my shoulder and pressed his hand hard against the glass door.

"Says open till nine," he said.

"I was closing early." I tried not to sound afraid.

"I'm only in town for the night. Wanted to get some ink."

"Um," I said. I looked at him. He wasn't any taller than I was, but he was burly and mean-looking, with crazy, red-rimmed eyes. His hair was streaked with gray, and so was his beard. The first image that came to mind was that of a very bad dog.

"Says open till nine," he said again.

I nodded, reached inside, turned on the lights, and held the door open. I shrank back as he walked past. He tilted his head and examined the flash on the walls. I scurried into the back room and watched him through the window.

"You do custom work?"

I nodded. The straight-edge razor was the closest thing to a weapon in the shop. There was no one I could call, except maybe 911, and nothing had happened yet. What was I supposed to say? There's a scary man in the tattoo shop? They'd just laugh.

"Let's get started." He came through the swinging doors, taking off his shirt. His torso was one big seascape, from his collarbone to his wrists, stretching across his chest and belly. Ships, mermaids, fish, pirates.

"What's your name?" I asked.

"You can call me Jim."

"Not much bare skin, Jim. What do you want?"

"Treasure chest. Right here." He pointed to a bare place on his chest.

I shaved his chest and drew a treasure chest on a rocky ledge. I added gems and coins spilling over the sides and trickling down into the mermaids' hair tattooed on his ribcage. "How's that?" I handed him a mirror and he examined the drawing.

"Perfect. Add a crown right there, on the corner, something you can make real sparkly."

After I added the crown and got out my tattoo machines, I noticed a skull with bulging eyeballs in the middle of a swirl of fish, low on his stomach. "Nice," I pointed. "Gil Monte do that?"

"Yep. I dig his style, not to mention it'd been a while since I'd got tattooed in a real shop, and I didn't find out till I seen him on TV that the guy who did it is some kind of famous. Most of the rest of what I got is jailhouse shit. See this mermaid? Got it in Chino. Guy made a tattoo gun from this Walkman motor and a guitar string. The ink, well, we burnt a few Styrofoam cups under a magazine, scraped off the black shit, and mixed it with toothpaste."

"That can't be a very good thing to put in your body," I said.

"In the joint," he said, "you just don't care. This here was my first one." He touched a crooked Old English "USMC" that had faded and spread. "Got it from a buddy in 'Nam. I was the only one in my unit who made it home."

I took my time tattooing the treasure chest. Impeccable shading, perfect color. The whole time I leaned over his chest, I was aware of his breath on my hair and the heat rising from his body. When I first saw him at the door, I would have given anything never to have had to touch him, but now I wanted to make sure Jim left my shop with the best tattoo I could do.

When it was finished, I handed Jim the mirror. He nodded and smiled.

"Scared you, didn't I," he said, buttoning his shirt.

"No."

"Yes I did."

"Maybe." I said softly.

"Admit it." He laughed. "You were thinking who you could call, what you could use as a weapon."

I was too ashamed to meet his eyes. "Sorry."

"Happens all the time," he said. "*All* the time."

"Maybe it does," I said, "but that doesn't make it right. And it's not at all okay that it happened in a tattoo shop. You're like what tattooing used to be, all the things that made tattoos so cool to the people who are getting them now, and if you can't even be treated decently in a tattoo shop, what's the world coming to?"

"Things change," Jim said softly. He shoved his hands into his pockets and looked away. His eyes looked rheumier than before, tears swelling at the corners.

"It was an honor to tattoo you," I said. I stuck out my hand, but he didn't take it. Instead, he smiled and wrapped his arms around me, squeezed me hard and close.

"The honor was mine." He held me out at arm's length, one hand on each of my shoulders. He wasn't smiling, but the tears were gone from his eyes.

SLADE HAD STOPPED in Los Angeles on the way home from Ace Tattoo in San Diego, and had—so far—spent a week with friends I'd never met. I was beginning to think that he was never coming back.

"Man, you wouldn't believe it. You just walk down the street here, nod at one of the guys leaning against the building. The guy nods back, you give him some money, and he spits a chunk of smack into your hand." Slade's voice on the phone, slurry in the middle of the night.

"So you're staying in one of the better neighborhoods, then?" I yawned and looked at the clock. Three A.M.

"I'm having a blast. You aren't going to believe what happened."

"Hmm." I yawned again.

"Remember Lauren?"

"Your girlfriend from Venice Beach?" I asked. "From way back?"

"Yeah. I got a wild hair the other day and called her up."

It turned out that whatever chemistry had burned between them ten years earlier had been resparked. Slade flew back to Laramie a few days later, glowing with an excitement I'd never seen before on his face. He stopped at the shop, threw a bunch of his stuff into boxes, loaded it into his car, and told me to come by his house after work. He said he had packing to do. He said we needed to talk.

A few hours later, I opened Slade's door and squeezed past the cat and a huge, half-finished model of a creature from *Alien*. Boxes were strewn everywhere, and he'd been pulling things off the walls and out of drawers and tossing them into the boxes haphazardly. He was taking a bong break, sitting cross-legged on his bed, looking very much like the caterpillar from *Alice in Wonderland*. He tossed me a tiny balloon, a treat from his California vacation, and I laid out a smallish line of heroin and snorted it. I lay down on the floor and began picking at the wax that held my hair extensions to my scalp. It wasn't long before I managed to pluck a chunk of the not-mine bangs loose. I rolled over and looked at it. It reminded me of a severed limb, and I thought of the dozens of other severed limbs stuck to my own hair and began picking at them with as much ambition as I could muster.

"What I don't understand," I mumbled, "is why I didn't turn out right." Another extension tore free, taking some of my own hair with it. "Look." I held it up.

"Hmm," Slade said. "You did turn out right."

"I mean normal."

"Who's to say what's normal?"

"Why didn't I turn out like my parents? Like my sister?" Black spiderwebs of not-mine bangs were curling and clinging to the tattoos on my arms. I closed my eyes and scratched my face. I groped for a handful of hair extensions and tickled my cheeks with the ends, thinking about the woman who had actually grown this hair, cut it off, and sold it. I imagined that she had had a pretty interesting life. Either very tragic, very O. Henry, or else she'd been a solid businesswoman. A hair farmer.

"If you want to look at it that way, I didn't turn out normal either," Slade said. "My family's just like yours. Even got the perfect sister. I told my mom from the time I was a little kid that I had rare blood, that's why I was different. She said I had the same blood as the rest of the family, but then years and years later, we found out I've got B-negative. My mom read some Japanese study about blood types and personality, and it said that B-negative people are artistic and eccentric, that they don't follow the same path as everyone else. Nonconformists."

"I'm B-negative, too."

"There you go then." Slade spread his arm in a grandiose gesture and smiled as though this was the definitive answer. "Besides," he added, "aren't you a Scorpio? B-negative Scorpio. I think you've got your answer right there."

He was definitely turning into the caterpillar from *Alice in Wonderland*, sprawled on the mushroom of his bed with a bong in one hand and a hookah-shaped cloud of smoke above his head.

"That's the answer? There's got to be more to it. Don't you think? I mean, there's got to be quite a few B-negative Scorpios in the world, and they can't all be tattooed. They're certainly not all lying on your floor snorting smack and pulling someone else's hair out."

"Sensation." The *s*'s spun and pulsed through the room, dripping like water off the walls. "Think about it," Slade said. "The straight life is boring. I'm not saying it's wrong, you understand. Plenty of people live like that. On the surface, they seem like the most successful people in the universe, but their kind of success eats away the part of them that is, I don't know, human. They're great with logic, man, a bunch of robots in suits, calculating the next move, the next goal. They're so focused on this that they don't even see a lot of what's around them, and they're missing out. There's so much to see and feel and do."

The backs of my eyeballs itched. I wondered if it would be possible to take them out, scratch the backs, and replace them in their sockets. Sensation. Slade was right. If you don't know what the farthest reaches of sensation can be like, imagine being on the verge of orgasm, the first time another person finessed your body to that state of being, when you didn't know how it would feel and you're half scared but too excited to make it stop. Later, you lie there in the pulsing aftermath of curled toes and pleasurable exhaustion, limp and dry-mouthed, but wet and sticky everywhere else, and all you can think about is how—and how soon—you can possibly recapture that feeling.

Sometimes you can get to the same place with your second orgasm, or your hundredth, but sooner or later you know what to expect, and the scary anticipation is no longer part of the experience. When you want this particular thrill no matter what, you learn to find it in nonsexual experiences, and pretty soon you'll stop at nothing to achieve it, because you've become a sensation junkie. You need this feeling, and you look for it. You look hard.

"It's not too late to go back," Slade said. "You just, uh, fix your hair, get those tattoos lasered off, buy some pantyhose, and you're there. If that's what you want. Find yourself a nice college boy and settle down. It's your choice, doll. You can have a simple life, ordinary, with no complications. But how much fun is that going to be? You want to grow old eating lunch at the country club and picking out drapes for the den? Or do you want to really live? This is your chance to not die bored."

"Rick died." Tears welled up in my eyes, and I wiped at them with a fistful of hair extensions.

"Yeah, but he didn't die bored," Slade said. "You doing okay, doll?"

"So-so," I said. "I think I'd feel a whole lot better if I could get in bed with you."

Slade untied my shoes and stretched my legs out on the floor. He gathered up the hair extensions and put them on the table by the bed in case, he said, I'd need them later. He

tucked a pillow under my head and covered me with his favorite quilt, leaned over and kissed my nose. " 'Night,
buddy," he said.

SLADE LEFT THE next day to work in a tattoo shop in Denver for a couple of weeks. He spent the same two weeks
drinking, and on the next-to-last night of his trip, totaled
his Chevelle on a city street, taking out a few parked cars
along the way. He was arrested with more than a little bit of
force, thrown in jail, and then taken to the hospital.

The day he got out of the hospital, he took a taxi to the
Denver airport, picked up Lauren, and rode a shuttle bus
to Laramie. He left the Chevelle in Denver. I never would
have thought it possible, but his adoration of that car paled
in comparison to his love for Lauren. That night, over martinis, he proposed and she accepted.

Lauren wanted to go to medical school at UC Davis,
which meant that I had two choices: buy the tattoo shop or
look for another job. I took out a loan and the Body Art
Workshop was mine. Slade packed up his entire life in less
than twenty-four hours, moved to Davis, California, got
an apartment with Lauren, and opened a new shop, the
Tattoo Zoo.

I wasn't sure I wanted the responsibility of owning a
business, and it wasn't just buyer's remorse or loneliness
for Slade. I was pretty sure I didn't want to tattoo for the
rest of my life, but I had absolutely no idea what I could
possibly do instead. After Slade left, I unlocked the door to
the tattoo shop that was now mine and gathered up the

catalogs and envelopes from the floor below the mail slot. Bills, mine now. The latest in tattoo equipment, also mine. An invitation to a ten-year high-school reunion. Mine.

I could ride on a float in the Jubilee Days parade, get reacquainted with old pals, and show off my school spirit, all at the same time, according to a letter that sounded personal but wasn't. In the unlikely event that I'd be unable to attend, the letter continued, Laramie High School's Class of '81 was counting on me to fill out the attached questionnaire and return it, along with a recent photograph. It felt like a pop quiz; at eighteen, what had I seen for my ten-years-older self, and where was I at twenty-eight?

I folded the letter and put it with Slade's forgotten odds and ends in a box I hadn't decided whether to ship, store, or throw out. I looked around the shop for a long minute, relocked the door, and walked up the block to the coffee place. I already had a case of the jitters, the kind you'd expect from a handful of trucker speed, but the only thing I wanted — for sure — was a triple-shot, low-fat latte.

Chapter Eleven

As seasons went, winter was the worst for business; it seem that people forget about their skin a little bit more with the addition of each layer of winter clothing. It was early December when the BODY ART WORKSHOP sign came down and GRIFFIN DERMAGRAPHICS went up. Other than the sign over the door, the tattoo shop was still the same place, more or less; the flash was just harder to find. The flash sheets were laminated in plastic, and Slade had stuck them to the wall with a nail on every corner. Long strips of black lath had been nailed over the horizontal seams, intersected by vertical seams that were punctuated with shorter pieces of the same stuff. I pulled hundreds of nails and put the flash into binders. I put the binders on the bottom shelf of a large bookcase, hidden beneath art books and illustrated books about mythology, the history of tattooing, and the meanings of things.

Once the lath and the design sheets came down, the walls looked more naked than bare, more tortured than texturized where the nails had been. I spackled and sanded and spackled some more. I stuck paint swatches everywhere and considered the changing nuances of a dozen shades of white in the winter sunlight for two weeks before I settled on an alabaster that was warm without being brazenly pink. I started painting one evening after the shop closed, and stopped after midnight with one wall to go.

I let myself into the shop earlier than usual the next morning, in a hurry to finish the walls before I opened for business. I'd barely begun painting when I had the distinct sensation of being watched. Not just watched, really, more like *examined.* I glanced over my shoulder and saw a man standing on the sidewalk, looking into the waiting room with more curiosity than most window-shoppers. I put down my brush, went into the tattoo room, and stared at him through a gap in the closed blinds.

He had his hands shoved into his pockets and the collar of his coat turned up against the wind. He was about my height, maybe a little taller, but not much. He had long, curly black hair pulled back into a ponytail, with wind-whipped tendrils brushing against his cheeks. His jaw was square, but his features were soft and rounded, generous lips punctuated by two dimples beneath gold-flecked hazel eyes. He looked sunny. There was no other way to describe it.

I sat down in the tattoo chair and picked up a magazine. Ever since Rick, I'd made up my mind to steer clear of men, sunny or otherwise. Fifteen minutes later, I peeked. He was still there, but it looked like the cold wind was starting to get to him. Another fifteen minutes passed. And another. Finally he was gone, and I was glad.

Six hours later, the winter twilight was suspended between dusk and dark beneath snow clouds and refracted lights. When the sunny man reappeared, he looked like an angel, his dark hair silhouetted by the streetlight and big white snowflakes on his head and jacket.

"I'm Paul," he said, holding out his hand. "I'm thinking about a tattoo," he said. "Homer Simpson, maybe, or a black cat."

"Karol." I smiled and shook his hand. "Please don't get a cartoon character. You'll regret it later."

"Even Homer Simpson?"

I scrunched up my face and we settled on a black cat. I drew it up, stenciled it, and put the stencil on his arm. He looked at it this way and that in the mirror while I got everything ready.

"Where are you from?" Paul asked.

"Here." I poured a cap of black ink and tore open a sterilization pouch.

"Wow. You don't look like it," he said. "I'm from California. San Francisco. Is this going to hurt?"

"Not much. The outline is the worst of it. What do you do in San Francisco?" I asked.

"I'm an attorney."

"Have a seat," I said, snapping on my latex gloves.

Paul sat down and I rolled my stool closer to the chair. He smelled good. I tried to ignore it. I blotted the stencil and dipped the needles into the ink. "I'm going to do one little bit of one little line, just so you know what to expect."

"Okay." He shut his eyes and gripped the arm of the chair.

I outlined the cat's tail. "Not bad?"

"Not nearly as bad as I expected." He looked at his shoulder, shuddered slightly, and asked if he was bleeding.

"Not much," I said.

"This isn't at all how I expected a tattoo shop to be," he said.

"Is this the first shop you've been in?"

"Yeah." Paul looked sort of sheepish, as though he thought I might have expected more.

"Why'd you decide to get tattooed?" I'd finished the outline and switched to my shader.

He shook his head. "You'll think it's stupid."

"Let me guess," I said. "You're not like all the other lawyers. You're a rebel."

"It's not that stupid," Paul said. "Or maybe it is. This morning I saw you walking across the street. I walked around the block a couple times and saw that you worked here, and I decided to get a tattoo because I couldn't think of any other way to meet you."

I patted his arm and laughed. Pretty soon, he was laughing, too. "You could have just come in and said hello. That's what most people do."

He tipped his head back and forth. "Yeah, but it's more of an adventure this way, don't you think?"

He was back the next day. "I found this story about tattoos. I thought you might like it." He stumbled over his words. Even though it was freezing out, he wore only a vest over his T-shirt. The tattooed cat was covered in a big glob of Neosporin. He held Flannery O'Connor's complete collection of short stories, outstretched in both hands, like an offering. "It's called 'Parker's Back'."

"I love Flannery O'Connor." I took a paper towel and wiped most of the Neosporin off his arm.

"Me, too." His big, beamy smile faded into an awkward silence. He shoved his hands into his pockets, rocked back and forth on his heels, and looked at the flash on the walls.

"My cousin, thrice removed, had a roommate who lived in Laramie," he said. "She told me about a bar here, one with dead animals on the wall and a bullet hole in the mirror."

"That would be the Buckhorn," I said. "It's just up the block and around the corner."

"Oh." Paul scuffed one boot against the other and looked up at the ceiling.

"Do you want me to go there with you?" I asked.

Another big, beamy smile, and five minutes later we were sitting in a booth at the Buck, drinking long-neck Budweisers and talking as though we'd known each other for a long, long time. After an hour or so, we went back to the tattoo shop. Paul wrote his name and telephone number on the last page of the Flannery O'Connor book.

"If you're ever in San Francisco…" He hugged me, smiled, and left.

I couldn't get him out of my mind. A week later, I wrote him a letter—typed a letter, to be precise, as though I followed up like this on every tattoo I did. I hoped that the impersonal presentation and aloof tone would lend the letter an air of customer service instead of desire. I hoped Paul liked me back. Our letters crossed in the mail. Paul's letter said that his tattoo was starting to itch, but he was braver than I on paper. "I'm glad," he wrote, "that we chanced upon one another."

I carried his letter with me everywhere, like a paper amulet, smoothing it out and rereading it endlessly. At home, at work, between tattoos. I wanted to tell someone about this, wanted to call Slade and read the letter aloud, but the letter and the sensation were so dear to my heart that I couldn't tell anyone without breaking the spell.

A week before Christmas a package arrived, wrapped in brown paper and addressed in handwriting that was tip-of-the-tongue familiar without conjuring a name or a face. The box contained wrapped presents—a pound of coffee, a bottle of bath oil, and *The Violent Bear It Away* by Flannery O'Connor. My heart was pounding as I dialed Paul's number.

"Hello?"

"Thanks for the package," I said. "Oh. This is Karol."

"I know. I was just thinking about you. I was thinking about coming back to Laramie."

"Why?" I asked.

"I want to see you."

$\mathcal{I}$T WAS THE MIDDLE of January and too cold to snow, a little more than two weeks until Paul's visit. I was in the back room of the tattoo shop, wrapped in a blanket, lying on the couch and watching *Oprah* on a TV set I'd turned on its side. A stack of overdue bills cluttered the desk. I hadn't tattooed anyone in more than a week, and I needed to make a hundred dollars a day in order to pay off my loan for the shop and keep up with my bills at home. In the summer I sometimes made four times that much, and I'd spent the first half of the afternoon berating myself for not knowing, by now, the importance of coming up with a budget and sticking to it. I'd spent the rest of the afternoon wondering what, exactly, was so great about that kind of self-discipline and watching other people bare the most intimate details of their lives on national TV.

The heat vents were in the ceiling. I stood on the counter from time to time to warm my hands; the heat clung to the upper layers of the shop air, suspended a foot or so from the ceiling. The storefront windows were iced over, and the draft around the back door let in frigid bursts of winter wind. The bells nailed to the front door startled me, and I dragged my blanket to the window between the tattoo room and the waiting area to see what was going on.

Six young people came into the shop, stomping their

snowy boots all over my carpet. I could tell that the two girls and at least one of the boys were underage. They whispered and giggled and whispered some more and nudged one of the older boys in my direction.

"I want a heart with a banner." He made a circle with his thumb and forefinger. "About so big. What's that going to run me?"

"Can I see your I.D.?" I held out a hand.

He pulled out his wallet and handed me a driver's license. He was eighteen. Barely. "How much?"

"What do you want in the banner?"

"Your name," he said. His entourage laughed.

"My name?"

"No, the words 'your name.'" He made quotation marks with his fingers.

"Uh-huh. And where do you want this tattoo?"

"On my butt."

"Why?" I asked.

"So I can win money," he said, as though that should have been obvious.

"What?"

"So I can go up to people in a bar and say, 'Hey, betcha fifty bucks I got your name tattooed on my ass.'" He looked so proud, and his friends laughed and laughed.

"Are you serious? You're not even old enough to get into a bar."

"Hell yes, I'm serious." He delivered this with an attempt at macho posturing.

The price of any tattoo was loosely based on an hourly rate with a minimum, usually determined by design size and body part. Stomachs, for instance, were more elastic and harder to stretch, and took much longer to tattoo than an arm or a leg. I did a quick heart-with-banner-plus-butt-time tally and came up with a forty-dollar price tag. The past-due bills, my empty refrigerator, and his attitude caused the price to double, and the inanity of it all bumped the final figure up into a nice round number.

"A hundred bucks," I said.

"A hundred dollars?" He sounded shocked.

"It'll be there forever. Really, it's only pennies a day." Sarcasm to me. Persuasion, apparently, to him.

"Okay, yeah, okay."

"Read this and sign it." I handed him a release form. "It'll take a few minutes for me to draw up the lettering." I went into the back and sat at the drafting table, trying to convince myself that it was his choice, not my responsibility.

The next three days passed without a single customer. No one even came in to look.

Saturday night meant Friday to me as far as my work week went. The tattoo shop was empty. The sun had set. I was sitting in the tattoo chair, sprawled out on it, actually, flipping impatiently through a magazine and waiting for nine o'clock to roll around so that I could turn the OPEN sign around. I put down the magazine and wondered whether I ought to dye my hair. I picked up the mirror next to the ink rack and studied the overprocessed fringe of my bangs, pondering potential colors.

Past time to pluck my eyebrows, I noticed. *Maybe I ought to get my teeth capped.* I smiled real big and tried to imagine my mouth framing a big white movie-star smile.

I looked at my nose and thought of piercing it myself. I found a pen and made a dot on my right nostril. That's where the hole would go, if I were going to do it, which I wasn't.

I scrubbed the day's tubes, bagged them in autoclave tubing, and put the bags in the tray. I found a small gold hoop in the tray of body-piercing jewelry that Slade had left behind and bagged it up, too. I cleaned the countertops and the floor. The autoclave popped open twenty minutes later.

I looked at the piercing forceps, nasty things with locking scissor handles and spoon-shaped ends with holes in the center. I wondered how much the forceps might hurt once they were locked closed on a piece of skin. I clamped them onto my nostril. *That's not so bad,* I thought. I tore open a sterile package and pulled out a wicked-looking piercing needle, hollow with a malevolent taper. I looked in the mirror, aligned the needle and the dot, and pushed. *That's not so bad,* I thought. *Not bad at all.* I didn't think the needle could be very far in, not past the first layer or so, because it didn't hurt a bit until I stabbed the inside of my septum and backed away, shrieking, from the mirror. When the tears dried up enough that I could see again, my nostril was neatly shish-kabobed.

As long as the needle is in there, I thought, *I might as well put the jewelry in.* I unclamped the forceps, tucked the gold hoop in the blunt end of the needle, and pulled it through. I wondered what body modification had come to, at least for me, when the combination of curiosity and boredom was reason enough to pierce something. I locked the clasp on the gold hoop and went back to the mirror. I hoped I'd like it. I didn't want to look like the biker chicks in tattoo magazines, those girls with a nose ring chained to an earlobe like a trucker's wallet to a belt loop. I wanted to look exotic. In the mirror, my red, pierced nose looked like something in between.

$\mathcal{I}$ DROVE TO DENVER in a raging blizzard to pick Paul up at the airport. On the drive home, he held his hand hesitantly above my thigh, not touching, just hovering there.

"Would it be okay if I touched you?" he asked. "I just want to make sure you're real."

I nodded, and he placed his hand lightly on my knee. He left it there for sixty miles.

He'd seen Laramie, and I wanted to show him the West, so after a week of hanging out in the tattoo shop, I decided to take Paul someplace special.

Once upon a time, a city boy named Owen Wister rode a train from the east coast to Medicine Bow and wrote

The Virginian, a classic western novel with a local setting. Since then, Medicine Bow had become the hub of a depressed mining and ranching community struggling to maintain a sense of decorum in the face of a brutal economy and an interstate that went in too far south.

Trains hadn't stopped in Medicine Bow for years, and people didn't read westerns much anymore. The trains that came through town didn't even slow down. They flew past, a blur of boxcars and coach windows on grumbling fast wheels, announced by piercing, mournful whistles and the solemn, ceremonial lowering of stiff-armed striped barricades across the dirt road on either side of the tracks. The railroad station was a museum in the summer, closed and boarded up during the long winter months. Out front was a weathered wooden sign recounting Wister's journey, *The Virginian,* and the history of Medicine Bow.

The hotel across from the railroad station was built in the 1920s and named after Wister's book. It was the tallest building in town, four stories of rusticated blocks of granite chiseled from nearby quarries. The first floor of the hotel was shared by the Virginian Cafe and the Shiloh Saloon. There was no lobby, no registration desk, just a cupboard of keys behind the café cash register. The café catered mostly to locals, but sometimes in the summer, families from out of state, traveling off the beaten path, stopped there, lured in by a billboard on the highway just past Como Bluff and the "Believe It or Not" fossil museum. The billboard has Wister's name in fancy script, along with one of the best-known one-liners in western

SIGN AT MEDICINE BOW, WYO.

literature: "When you call me that, smile." The tourists who stopped in Medicine Bow poked around the railroad museum and ate lunch in the café, wandering through the hotel while their hamburgers were on the grill.

The second floor was arranged almost like a museum. Each room was different but they all had handmade quilts and porcelain washbasins on the dressers and sepia photographs. The Owen Wister Suite was the only room with its own bath; the others shared a "water closet" in the hall. The rooms were all unlocked, doors wide open, with tarnished ropes of brassy chain link hanging across the doorways. With family pride and small-town trust, no one monitored the rooms or the pockets of tourists when they left.

"WEREN'T YOU UP HERE a few summers ago?" One of the waitresses eyed my tattoos in a way that was both suspicious and friendly. The café waitresses, three heavyset lookalikes with short, permed hair, swarmed around the booth, touching my purple hair. They stared openly.

"I've been here before," I said, and smiled.

The waitresses left Paul and me to our steaks and Budweisers, and squeezed into a booth across the room. It was Saturday night, the dinner rush had come and gone, and the sounds of the jukebox were warming up the weekend crowd next door at the Shiloh Saloon. The waitresses' conversation filled the room, and I thought I overheard their names: Curly, Jo, and Mary. Could that be right?

"I told you we was baking too many potatoes."

"How the hell was I supposed to know it would snow this much?"

"If they plow the roads by morning, maybe we can get us a decent breakfast crowd."

They talked about men and dirty dishes and whose turn it was to do them. All three, to hear them tell it, would be waking up with two pairs of boots under the bed. All three were looking for a ticket out of Medicine Bow.

"Small towns make you bitter," Curly said. The other two nodded knowingly, and smoke rose from matching cigarettes in a shared ashtray, like a smoldering secret.

$\mathscr{P}$AUL AND I PICKED up the key to the Owen Wister Suite at the café cash register when we paid for our dinner. We navigated a maze of tables to the stairs, just past the kitchen. The worn floral carpeting and old-fashioned mural on the landing made me think of all the feet that had come up these same stairs. I thought that, maybe, if we were quiet enough, we could hear the past, the passengers getting off the train and carrying trunks to their rooms. Maybe we'd hear Owen Wister's fountain pen as he scratched notes about the people and the place, Medicine Bow seen through turn-of-the-century city-boy eyes.

We explored the suite, all its nooks and crannies, the tiny warped drawers in the rolltop desk. Sounds from the café kitchen and the Saturday-night crowd in the saloon were distant and cheerful, muffled now and then by gusts

of wind howling around the corners of the building. The
red flashing lights of the railroad crossing and the lone
bright yellow headlights of the passing trains were reflected,
refracted, on the icy night windows.

The bathroom was a warm cubbyhole just off the bedroom, a step up onto plush new red carpet, a closet before
the plumbing moved indoors, with a claw-foot bathtub big
enough for two, hot water gushing from the old-fashioned
spigot. Paul and I sat in the dark, rubbing soap on each other
and letting the suds run through our fingers. We talked about
our lives, our futures, and the months that comprised our
common past. Our time together seemed shorter and more
fragile in a sixty-year-old bathtub; everything dreamy seemed
vulnerable, but that didn't matter much because the vulnera-
bility of being in love was so dreamy.

The sounds of the saloon were louder in the bathroom, wafting up through the overworked heating system
that vented near the tub. Calling to us.

The bartender had worked at the Shiloh for years, had
been in Medicine Bow as long as I could remember. His
face was sweet and open, lined and leathery, and he walked
with a limp that seemed more charming than tragic as he
rustled up a couple of long-neck Buds for me and Paul. He
watched with unconcealed amusement as I gave Paul the
magic snake ring from my left index finger and Paul traded
me the shirt off his back. We wanted to give each other
everything, anything, to prove the feeling that paled in our
words. I love *you,* I *love* you, *I* love you, *I love you.* Language

wasn't enough because we'd both said those words before, too many times to too many people.

"Can I get change for the jukebox?" Paul asked, sliding a dollar across the bar.

"Can't play the juke after eleven. Got people stayin' up-stairs tonight." The bartender pointed to the ceiling and pushed the dollar back. Paul and I looked at each other with big, delighted smiles.

"But that's us!" Paul laughed, and the bartender smiled back, gave us a handful of quarters, limped across the room, and plugged in the jukebox. The bar was almost empty, and it wasn't even midnight. An old man hovered near our bar stools, his stooped shoulders and stiff bowlegs giving away his occupation before he opened his mouth.

"I'm Billy Ray," he said, pumping our hands. "Just an old cowboy, *you* understand." His eyes twinkled in a field of crumply wrinkles, evidence of a life spent squinting into the sun and years of hard living. We traded stories with Billy Ray, and laughed comfortably as he dished out a bit of old-fashioned cowboy ribbing to the city boy. I was exempt from this half-serious contempt for all things urban be-cause I grew up just down the road, but Paul was from Cal-ifornia. I couldn't keep my eyes off Billy Ray's fingers as they fidgeted with his lips and white white WHITE mus-tache, trying to hide the dentist's clear-cut handiwork.

"Left 'em in an arena in Amarillo," Billy Ray explained behind a fluttering leathery paw. "That old Brahma went left and I went right, ended up in the dust with a mouthful of hoof. Kind of bashful talking without 'em. *You* understand." He smiled shyly, a flash of pink gums that faded into a friendly arc of puckering lip-flesh.

I played Patsy Cline over and over, all the old sad songs that are neither so old nor so sad when you're in love, song after country song on scratchy 45s.

One of the café waitresses, maybe Mary, danced with Billy Ray. She threw her head back, laughing gleefully each time he spun her out and pulled her close again. I watched over Paul's shoulder, my hands on the soft, bare skin underneath his jacket. We were hugging more than dancing, our bodies melting into one another and swaying from side to side. When the song ended, I went to the jukebox for more. Billy Ray stopped me at the end of the bar and pressed three sweaty quarters into my hand.

"Play that one again, sweet thing," he said. I played it again, over and over, for Billy Ray and because I was in love.

I go out walking after midnight and *all my exes live in Texas.* Billy Ray's from Texas, just an old cowboy, you understand, teeth kicked in by a bull. *Crazy for feeling so lonely without you.*

When the bar closed, Paul and I tiptoed through the dark café and crept up the stairs, whispering even though there was no one to disturb. The open doorways of the second-floor rooms looked both sinister and inviting. The brassy chains glinted in the light from the hall and swayed slightly, shaking from the movement of passing trains or unseen hands. We pulled at one another's clothes before we reached our room, ducked under eight brass-and-velvet chains and rumpled the bedclothes on eight hotel beds.

There was no one but me and Paul on the second floor, no one but me and Paul in the whole world. I ran up and down the hallway in my underwear, thinking, *I'm the happiest girl in the whole USA.*

Trains became seductive, climactic. Eight beds later, giggling and sighing, we were back in Owen Wister's feather bed. Paul was silhouetted above me, and the moaning of the train whistle mixed with my own. For a moment, Paul's face was unexpectedly illuminated, smiling and passionate. I wanted to freeze that moment forever. I could have stayed just like that, Paul smiling, me smiling, forever.

Chapter Twelve

"I'M GETTING married," I told Slade.

"To the lawyer?"

"Yes."

"I see." A good two minutes of silence on the telephone line, and finally Slade's long-distance sigh.

"I love him," I said, and started to pace my apartment, dragging the phone behind me. I was surrounded by tattoos and art. Colored pencils and tattoo magazines were scattered across my desk, and the walls were covered with my photographs of tattooed people. I was the subject in the few pictures I didn't take. Me tattooed. Me tattooing. Me. Slade and I had been friends for close to ten years, a not-quite decade that had changed my life and my skin forever. He'd known me in love and out, but we'd never been in love with each other, at least not in the usual sense of the phrase.

"Is the lawyer moving to Laramie?" Slade asked.

"No." I pulled the phone onto the sloping plywood balcony outside my living-room window and propped my leg on the railing, aligning the black stripes of my Raggedy Ann stockings with the white balustrades. "I'm moving to San Francisco. That's where he lives."

"What about the tattoo shop?"

"Selling it," I said softly, the first time I'd said it out loud. I pressed the phone hard to my ear, but the only sound on the other end was Slade's breathing. "I love him," I said again.

"Of course you do. And you know what? I love him for you. It's too late, that's all. Maybe five years ago, you could have pulled this one off, but not now."

"Everything will be just fine." I shifted the phone to my left ear. I didn't like Lauren any more—or any less—than I'd liked any of Slade's other girlfriends, which meant that I knew how Slade felt about Paul, even though the two of them had never met. It wasn't jealousy so much as an annoyed feeling anytime either of us had to give up whatever part of our friendship an interloper seemed to demand.

"Are you going to work in Frisco?" Slade asked.

"I'm sure I can find something."

"You know what I'm asking. Are you going to tattoo?"

"Of course not." I was going to be married. I wanted to be a wife, which was one thing Slade didn't know about me, and I had certain ideas about what being a wife involved, which was another. The wife I was going to become would collect casserole recipes and *Good Housekeeping* magazines. Tattoos wouldn't matter one way or the other to the kind of wife I'd be, a wife whose life before marriage would be trivial at best when compared to wedded bliss.

"You think you can do it like that? Just walk away from tattooing? You can't, doll. Don't you see that you're already committed to something that is the exact opposite of his lifestyle?"

"You and Lauren are getting married," I said.

"Yeah, but I'm still tattooing," Slade said. "How long are you going to be happy being June-fucking-Cleaver? Save yourself some heartache and get out while you can."

"I think you might be wrong," I said.

"So, for the sake of argument, let's play it your way. You're not a tattoo artist anymore. Fine. What kind of job are you going to get? Waitress? Secretary?"

"It doesn't matter," I said. "I love him."

"It's going to matter," Slade said. "It's going to matter a lot."

A MONTH BEFORE the wedding, Paul called me late at night from San Francisco.

"You know your nipple rings?" he said. "I don't like them."

"I see," I said. "You realize now that you have lost your breast privileges completely. What do you expect me to do? Take them out?"

"Well, yes," he said.

"I'll give it some thought." I hung up without saying good-bye, and the phone rang again.

"What's the big deal?" Paul asked. "Why can't you just take them out?"

"Maybe I just don't want to," I said.

"If we break up," Paul offered, "I'll pay for you to get them repierced."

"I don't think so." I hung up again.

It was a few days before I was done being mad, a few days before I could discuss my nipples without yelling or crying. Paul was a lawyer, but I still thought he was wrong for trying to negotiate with the person he was supposed to love more than anything else in the world. It took the romance out of compromise. A week later, I took out my nipple rings. The pierced skin closed up almost immediately, as though the jewelry had never been there.

My parents were quite pleased with my decision to marry Paul. They believed that I was finally back on track. In my father's eyes, this made up for many of my past mistakes, especially when I told him that I was selling the tattoo shop—hanging up my guns, as it were—and moving to California to be a wife.

Six months after Paul and I met, a roomful of strangers gathered in the parlor of the Owen Wister Suite at the Virginian Hotel in Medicine Bow, Wyoming. A tattooed bride, a Methodist minister, a Shiloh Saloon bartender best man, a Jewish groom, and a teenage maid of honor I'd never met before. The walls were covered with flocked red wallpaper and bordello lacy drapes, and the rumble of the freight trains across the highway drowned out most of the ceremonial words. I wouldn't have wanted to get married anyplace else.

"Do you, Karol, take Paul to be your wedded husband?" the Methodist minister asked.

"I do," I said, and Paul slid a ring onto my finger.

BEFORE I ARRIVED in San Francisco, Paul rented an apartment for us in the Mission District, a block from the law firm where he worked. It was a sunny third-floor flat in a building with a once-elegant Moroccan-style lobby and a heavy, wrought iron security door. The Mission District was either a quaint barrio or a dangerous ghetto, depending upon your mood, your gender, and what part of the neighborhood you were passing through. English was a second language—sometimes not even that—in the stores and on the streets. Everything was *en Español*. My Spanish was limited to nasty slang picked up in the neighborhood and fleeting memories of a junior-high Spanish class, but I liked shopping in the local markets. Pasta at Lucca's, vegetables from the open-air stand in front of the Lucky Pork grocery, and bread from a place on Valencia.

One afternoon, I went to a meat market on Mission Street to buy chicken. I explained in English that I wanted two chicken breasts. I pointed. The man behind the counter pointed from his side at everything except chicken and said, "*Esta?*" I decided to make an effort to communicate in Spanish.

"*Dos chi chis de pollo,*" I said, and smiled nicely to apologize for my rotten accent. The woman next to me explained in a stage whisper that I had ordered chicken tits. Two of them. I shopped at the Safeway on Market Street after that.

For Paul's birthday, I gave him a bolo tie that had belonged to my great-uncle. Weeks earlier, I had made reservations for dinner at an expensive restaurant that Paul's friends had recommended. When we got there, the maître d' blocked our way into the dining room. The restaurant had a strict dress code, he explained, which meant that men must wear suit coats and ties.

"I *am* wearing a suit coat and tie," Paul said.

The corners of the maître d's mouth turned so far down that I thought they were going to meet under his chin when he looked at the bolo hanging around Paul's neck. We compromised by sitting at a dusty corner table in the bar. My chair was directly beneath a hanging planter; the maître d' held aside a handful of half-dead fern fronds so that I could duck and shuffle my way to my seat. He let go with a flourish, leaving me with a hula-skirt halo of dried leaves.

I ordered the *pollo al mattone,* flattened chicken with rosemary and garlic, because it was the only entrée that didn't come on a "bed" of something. The chicken looked like roadkill, a nondescript pile of flattened meat and broken bones. I had eaten only a few bites before a cockroach dropped onto my shoulder from the hanging planter. It crawled on me for a moment, skittered across my plate, and then flew to a neighboring unoccupied table. The maître d' picked up a folded linen napkin, squashed the cockroach with a practiced flourish, and carried the napkin and its gory contents away. It was hard to get excited about eating out after that.

Ｗithout Ｗyoming, without tattooing, I was lost. I missed the person I used to be, missed the place I used to live. Homesickness, sadness, and anxiety ate away at my cheerful-wife façade until what Paul saw, more often than not, was a bundle of insecurities held loosely together by raw nerves. I'd never felt more naked in my life. I wanted comfort, solace, but I could tell by the look in his eyes that Paul felt deceived. This, certainly, was not what he'd married.

Without being able to refer to me as a tattoo artist, Paul's illusion became a bit tarnished. I was just a freaky-looking wife with dilettante skills, no goals, and minimal expectations. He began to sound more and more like my father, urging me to find some direction in my life. I began acting like my mother, fussing with the kitchen and the laundry and trying to make myself useful.

I flaunted my tattoos whenever it pleased Paul, wearing tank tops or sheer punk dresses when he wanted to impress his friends or shock his family. I kept them covered most of the rest of the time, as though that would keep me from turning into what I felt I'd become, which was something like Donna Reed on a bad acid trip.

Slade and I didn't see each other in person during this time, even though we were both living in California. The Tattoo Zoo was doing well, I heard. Slade and Lauren were still engaged, even though the wedding date kept moving farther into the future. More secondhand news. I didn't visit him at his new tattoo shop in Davis, mostly because I couldn't bear to be reminded of the life I'd left behind. Slade didn't visit me either, even though he came to San Francisco quite often. I didn't know if he felt betrayed or embarrassed on my behalf, but I was certain that he knew how things were turning out, and that he didn't want to hear about the sadness, because he could have told me — did tell me, in fact — that this is exactly what I should have expected.

𝒫AUL HAD A DIFFERENT sense of value, foreign priorities, and an oddly urban pride. "Have you ever seen anything like this?" He'd point with such pride that it didn't matter whether the question was rhetorical or not. He asked over and over until it didn't even matter whether he'd already pointed out the same maze of elevated freeways spiraling through skyscrapers. Or traffic jams so complicated that a river of red brake lights flowed as far as the eye could see. Or homeless eccentrics muttering as they wandered from gutter to dumpster, spare-changing passersby and clutching their worldly goods in a single battered paper bag.

"Have you ever seen anything like this?" Paul asked as thoug hI was from an underdeveloped country, another planet, a vacuum.

Every time I left the house, I felt my face contort into the mask of a city person, blank and emotionless, but a little scared around the eyes and as hard as possible around the mouth. I was not accustomed to living in a place where people avoid eye contact. Where I came from, people wave at strangers they pass on the road.

I was working in a downtown office building with fluorescent lights and artificial air and windows that didn't open. Autumn had come and gone with no noticeable change in climate. My feet hadn't touched dirt or grass in months, and I was relieved when Paul suggested getting out of the city, even though it was only for the day. We climbed into a minivan with a couple of his friends and headed for Mount Diablo.

"You'll like this," Paul said. "It's a lot like Wyoming."

Mount Diablo was sixty-five miles and three hours of bumper-to-bumper traffic away. We drove through cities and suburbs and subdivisions on six-lane roads and four-lane roads and two-lane roads. I kept waiting for it to feel like "out of the city," but then we reached the cul-de-sac housing developments clumped at the base of Mount Diablo and I had a pretty good idea that this wasn't going to be anything like Wyoming. We waited impatiently in a line of cars at the entrance to the "recreation area." A man in a green toll booth charged five dollars per car to pass through.

I'd never seen a mountain that people have to pay to touch, but Paul didn't think to ask me about that one, so I didn't mention it.

A two-lane road wound from the toll booth to the top of the mountain. The road was glutted with cars swerving around people in lycra and spandex with fanny packs and bottled water, people who had parked their cars at the bottom and were hiking or biking up the blacktop.

After a picnic lunch next to the Porta-John halfway up the mountain, we drove to the observation tower at the peak. Inside the observation tower was a collection of exhibits recounting the history of Mount Diablo. Stuffed birds and wildlife were posed beside plastic foliage and painted creeks. A tape of chirping birds and babbling brooks was piped through tinny speakers. Pictures of miners with shovels and picks lined a display of ore and rocks. A colorful mural illustrated the geological composition of the mountain, layer by scientific layer. A monochromatic display of arrowheads and pot shards was arranged in a dim corner near the exit, beneath a placard explaining the spiritual significance of Mount Diablo to the Native American tribes who lived here before the miners and city planners and cul-de-sacs took over.

We went outside and pushed our way through the crowded observation deck to catch a glimpse of the view. I thought I could see Sacramento, but it was hard to tell where one city ended and the next began. I could see the ocean, and beyond the smog of the Central Valley, I could make out the jagged mounds of the Sierras. From the observation deck, we had a close-up view of the forest of antennas and communication towers that blanketed the side of the mountain. The towers leaned at odd angles and the antennas looked as though they had been stabbed into the mountainside. Mount Diablo didn't remind me of Wyoming so much as it reminded me of a wounded animal waiting to die.

By 1995, THE MAGIC that had drawn us together was overshadowed by the horrific reality of what "till death do you part" might mean. We'd been married less than three years. We tried to get the magic back, as though it had been lost or stolen instead of thrown away. We reminded each other of the good intentions behind our whirlwind romance and impulsive marriage, and freely admitted our most obvious faults—my fearful irritation about living in a strange and hostile city, Paul's petulance about my lack of appreciation for it all—as though the city was to blame. As though geography was the problem.

Later that year I told Paul that I was going back to Wyoming, married or not. Much to my surprise, Paul agreed to come with me, even though he looked like I had suggested having him hog-tied and branded. He asked if he made me unhappy. I tried to explain that it wasn't him, that I just wasn't cut out to live in the city.

"You," Paul said, "never made an effort."

 $\mathcal{B}$ Y THE TIME we moved back, Laramie had swollen into something I barely recognized as my hometown. You could see from the shaggy line of the city limits which ranchers had sold out to developers and which ranchers hadn't. Paul adopted one western thing after another as his own, and bought whatever he needed to costume his new persona. First, there was the Resistol 10x beaver-felt cowboy hat. The hat never fit quite right because he didn't wear it enough to break it in, didn't want it marred by any sort of weather. The hat never lost its newness, never smelled more personal than the box it came in. He bought a pickup, a little four-cylinder two-wheel-drive Ford Ranger, because, he said, he wasn't living in Wyoming without a truck. He collected western words and phrases, peppered his speech with colloquialisms, and affected a drawl. Any stream of running water was a crick; concrete slabs, sidewalk or otherwise, were *cee*ment and worth talking about. He mimicked an accent I didn't know I had.

The novelty of all this wore off after six months or so, and Paul's affected drawl began to limn what he'd lost by moving to Laramie — decent Thai restaurants, for instance — more than anything he'd found.

In July, I loaded a picnic lunch and Paul into my car. I drove out of town, toward Centennial, and turned south when I got to North Fork. The road wound through widely spaced cabins and dense stands of chaparral and evergreens, broken by unexpected patches of willows and sage pastures. I watched carefully for the unmarked turn. I almost missed it, causing Paul to tip a little bit to one side when I slammed on the brakes and cranked the steering wheel.

"Sorry," I said. I turned onto a rutted road that wound up the side of the mountain. As we climbed higher, the road narrowed until it was no wider than the car. One side of the road hugged a wall of rock that rose steeply and looked dangerously close to crumbling. The other side fell sharply away to a creek.

"What happens if someone is coming from the other direction?" Paul asked.

I shrugged. "Someone has to back up." This wasn't going as well as I had hoped. I pulled over at the edge of an unfenced pasture and parked next to a NO TRESPASSING sign.

"We're stopping here?" Paul asked.

"Yes."

"But—" He pointed at the sign. I dismissed it with a wave of my hand. I got out, grabbed the picnic, and closed my door.

"You coming?" I asked.

"Are you sure it's okay to park here?"

"Don't worry. It's fine." I crossed the road and climbed to the top rail of a wooden gate festooned with a newer, larger NO TRESPASSING sign.

"What are you doing?" Paul sounded very concerned.

"Getting to the mountain."

"But you're trespassing. And it says right there not to." He pointed at the sign.

"Nobody's home. If they were, the gate wouldn't be locked." I tucked the toe of my shoe into a heavy chain that wrapped around the gate and the fence post, secured with a heavy, shiny padlock. I jingled it up and down. "See? Besides, all we have to do is go from here to that barbed-wire fence over there. Then we'll be on public land. It's hardly even trespassing. Two seconds, and we'll be way over there." I stared at him until he sighed and walked over to the gate. I jumped into the yard and casually pushed over a TRESPASSERS WILL BE SHOT sign before Paul had a chance to see it.

Paul loped across the yard and slipped through the barbed-wire fence on the other side. I took my time. "There," I said when we were both on the Forest Service side of the fence, "that wasn't so bad, was it?"

We walked up the old mining road, nothing more than two ruts, overgrown with weeds, which disappeared from time to time in the underbrush. We climbed for a mile or so, and the path leveled out and turned north. We crossed a shallow creek; I went first, hopping from log to rock to shore. I waited on the far side, encouraging Paul with a smile. When he stepped into the creek, he shattered the reflections of the sun and the mountain. He tried to step onto a boulder, but his wet loafer slipped off. His arms flailed wildly, and I covered my mouth with my hands to keep from laughing. Shimmers and sparks of water dripped

from his feet as he trampled a small patch of wild straw-
berries on the bank.

The trail ended abruptly in a tangle of windfall aspen.
We picked our way over the unstable trees and emerged on
top of my favorite slag. Paul walked out to the rim. Shale
trickled from his loafers to the bottom of the pile. A string
of puffy white clouds floated across the sky, headed south-
east, bright white against the blue. They left momentary
dark shadows on the prairie, shadows shaped like inkblots
and freshwater pearls.

"You can see forever," he said. "It's beautiful."

I began to unpack the lunch, laying out a tablecloth
and wighting the corners down with rocks. "It's the most
sublime place I know," I said. "Enough to make a person
believe in God, especially if you're already leaning in that
direction."

"Come on over and take a look," Paul said.

I shook my head. "That's okay," I said. "I don't like the
edges of things."

SUMMER ENDED. Leaves fell from the trees, snow began to
pile in drifts, and Paul disappeared into a cloud of unhappi-
ness. He didn't like Laramie. He didn't feel well. The relent-
less fog of his melancholy sucked me in, and each evening
ended with arguments and slammed doors. The quiet little
hurts punctuated by *you always* or *you never* led to long, tense
periods of misery, where we couldn't bear to be in one another's company but couldn't bear to be apart, either.

I loved Paul the most the mornings I woke before he did. I loved him the most before words got in the way, which happened more often than not whenever we woke up at the same time. I'd sit up slowly, careful not to disturb him, and watch him sleep, my arms wrapped around my knees. When he began to stir, I'd lean over and breathe in his warm, musky morning smell, lean farther until my face was on the pillow next to his before inching closer until I could feel the shape of his lips parting in a still-asleep smile beneath my kiss. For a few minutes, the friction that would push us apart later in the day (and would have started sooner, right that second even, if he'd been awake) was dormant. Sometimes, when we argued in the evening, and I found myself hating him—or me, or both of us—I'd go to bed early and cry myself to sleep, waiting to wake up and love him again.

Paul decided to move to Boise after two years in Laramie. I didn't want to go anywhere. He left for Idaho in May, and the plan was that I'd join him there at some unspecified point in the future. I tried to believe that Paul and I just needed a break from one another, that everything would work out just fine if we had a little time apart to reassess the situation, but that wasn't true. The seven-hundred miles between us was a separation in more than a geographical sense.

On our fourth wedding anniversary, Paul sent me roses from Boise and my attorney sent him a sheaf of legal papers dissolving our marriage. This, I thought, was one of our biggest problems—never wanting the same thing at the same time.

Chapter Thirteen

LARAMIE HAD TWO tattoo shops in 1997. The older one was where the Body Art Workshop had always been, but I'd never been inside. There were two artists, I'd heard from Slade. The owner was a man who'd been fired from at least one apprenticeship and eschewed everything traditional about the tattoo industry as a result. His apprentice was a young mother whose talent had eclipsed his own within a few months; this disequilibrium left him prone to fits of brutal petulance and temper tantrums in the presence of customers. The newer shop, Acme Tattoo, was a mile north of my house, a straight shot on a crooked path through the park. When I walked into Acme that first time, two big dogs rushed toward me, wagging tails and tongues. A man was sitting in a hydraulic hairdresser's chair behind a desk in the corner, and he was watching two young women examine the flash on the walls one sheet at a time with a smile that oscillated between flirtation and contempt. His eyes were hidden behind mirrored sunglasses.

I played with the dogs until the customers left, wiped my hands on my skirt and walked across the room. "I'm—"

"You're Karol." The hydraulics of the beauty-shop chair were testing their upper limits, but his legs still reached the floor. He was wearing overalls and big work boots. His dark hair hung in curls and waves to his shoulders, and he reached for my hand. "I've heard a lot about you. I'm John."

"I've got dog-slobber hands," I said. "Sorry."

"That's okay." He took my hand in his and smiled. "I like dog-slobber hands."

We talked for ten minutes. I started working the next day.

In the four years I'd been away from tattooing, it had become trendier than I'd ever have thought possible. Acme Tattoo was busy, but the tattoos we did were mostly flash, nothing personal, very small and very visible. Many of the customers lacked the depth of interest in the art form (and, I suspected, the attention span) for extensive tattoo work, but they appreciated it on other people, especially on John and me.

Most of John's tattoos were jailhouse work, the style and the sentiment so obvious that the question wasn't *whether* he'd done time (or even how much, unless one felt compelled to quantify "quite a bit"), but *where* or *for what*.

His favorite tattoo arced along the top of his belly, "OUT-LAW" in Old English lettering. He'd done it himself, up-side down in a jail cell, and the way he talked, it was as much a harbinger of his future as a reminder of his past. It summed up both his experiences and his beliefs. It was a tattoo to live by, six beautifully crafted, elaborately serifed letters spelling out the title of the book of John.

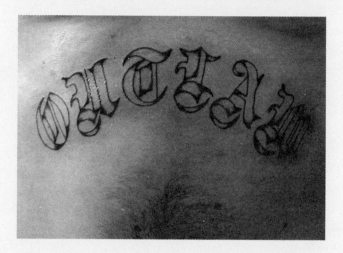

His initials were tattooed down the back of his left arm in a similar style, matched on the back of his right arm by FTW, like someone else's monogram.

"Most people," John said, "think it means 'Fuck the world.' But to a real biker, it means 'Forever two wheels.'"

"You have a motorcycle?" I asked.

"Uh, no. Not at present."

"Guess we'll have to go with 'Fuck the world,' then," I said.

"Are you trying to piss me off?"

"Nope," I smiled. "Just got lucky." I could see John replaying the conversation in his mind, and I was wondering whether I'd joked myself out of a job after less than two weeks, but his frown faded away and he laughed out loud.

That was the first time he kissed me. I still don't know what it meant. Before I had a chance to ask, two girls and a boy came into the shop. They milled around the front room, talking excitedly about the flash designs, and then gathered in a semicircle on the floor at my feet.

The boy, who couldn't have been more than twenty and was wearing a Nine Inch Nails T-shirt, pointed at my tattered paperback copy of *After Such Pleasures* on the arm of the couch.

"I just love Dorothy Parker," he said.

"Have you read much of her stuff?" I asked.

"None of it, actually. But I saw the movie. God, Jennifer Jason Leigh is so hot." He fell backwards, clutching his heart.

"You know who else is good?" One of the girls borrowed a cigarette from John and choked on the smoke as she lit it. "Burroughs." Her bangs were held back from her forehead by two plastic barrettes, bright fuchsia in the shapes of bows against shingled hair dyed lemon yellow.

"Burroughs is the greatest," the boy said. "I hope he never dies."

"He's dead," I said.

"No." The boy gasped and clutched his heart again.

"Yes."

"No." The barrette girl was on the verge of tears.

"Six months ago. Heart. Dead." I felt smug.

"Is Jack Kerouac dead, too?" The other girl's voice was soft and mewly. "I really like him."

A knot of irritation began forming in my stomach. "Since 1969," I said. "You don't need a tattoo. You need a library card."

John watched it all from the couch, laughing quietly and shaking his head.

THE NEXT DAY, I was standing in the doorway of the tattoo shop when John roared into the parking lot on a tricked-out Harley. I caught myself wondering whose motorcycle it was, and decided that it didn't matter.

"Hey," he said. "Want to go for a ride?"

The long, slim skirt I was wearing was hardly appro-

priate, but John revved the throttle without waiting for an answer, and I pulled up my skirt and slid on behind him.

We headed north on Ninth Street, which turned into Roger Canyon Road as soon as it hit the landfill and a cluster of ranchettes. John took a curve low and fast, and I held on to his waist. The wind whipped against my bare legs and blew my hair off my face. I looked over his shoulder at the speedometer. Eighty-five miles an hour.

If we wreck, I thought, *my head is going to split open like a ripe cantaloupe. At the very least, I am going to leave every skin cell from this leg on the asphalt, tattoos and all.* My only hope, in a crash, was that John would be thrown off first and I'd be lucky enough to land on top of him. This sparked a few other thoughts, spurred on by the vibrations of the motorcycle and the realization that my crotch was separated from John by nothing more than a thin layer of flowered cotton underwear. My breath caught in my throat when I saw the two of us in the circle of the rearview mirror. I looked happier than I could remember, happier than I'd been in years. We smiled at our reflections and the wind braided our hair together.

An hour later, we were winding through residential streets on the west side of the tracks, headed for a smoky little bar. John backed the motorcycle against the curb across from the shotgun cottage where Rick used to live. Besides boarding up the windows, nobody had done anything to the place. Maybe someone in Rick's family had had the place appraised, this rundown house on a narrow lot in the least desirable part of town, and maybe it wasn't worth the heart-wrenching task of sorting through Rick's things. Maybe twenty square feet of city property was nothing compared to the ranch they'd lost one subdivision at a time, or maybe they'd just forgotten about it. Or maybe Rick hadn't ever gotten around to telling them he owned a house in town, which seemed the most likely explanation. The yard was a weedy, gone-to-seedy garden of rusted car parts, blanketed with tumbleweeds and overgrown with thistles. His Cordoba was parked on the lawn, aspen runners snaking up through the engine compartment and peeking through the hood, which was leaning akimbo. All four tires were flat, the sides bleached and splayed open by years of sun and snow, and petals of corrosion blossomed around the bullet holes that ran the length of the passenger side.

John caught me staring. "You know who lives here?"

"Sort of," I said. "I used to. Yeah."

"Your buddy might want to think about a new lawn-care program, maybe get a Weed-Eater or something." John stopped and stared. "Hey, check it out, there's bullet holes in his car."

"Yeah." I nodded and kept walking, remembering the night Rick shot up his own car, the horrified look on my face, the way he shrugged the whole thing off instead of admitting that we'd been pissed as hell at each other right before he got the gun out. *It's all fun and games till someone loses an eye,* that's what he had said.

"Your friends are just like mine," John laughed and trotted to catch up. "It doesn't even faze you. I say bullet holes and you just nod, like why *wouldn't* his car be all shot up? Can't wait to meet the dude."

𝓐 FEW WEEKS LATER, John and I ran into each other at the kind of club neither of us would have been caught dead in had we been left to our own devices. We'd both arrived at Ground Zero as parts of separate couples. We'd both ditched our dates. We sat side by side at the bar, watching a girl on the dance floor who was bustin' a move, thrusting and swaying, a go-go dancer gone bad. She was surrounded by a throng of candy-assed, middle-class punks smoking clove cigarettes and swaying to and fro in a maelstrom of melancholia. The tattoo on her belly was the center of everyone's attention, a tribal circle of delicate lines.

Closer to the spotlights and the mirrored ball was a girl determined to be pretty. She was wearing an expensive leather miniskirt and a black bikini top, and her makeup was straight out of the pages of the latest *Vogue,* delicate eyeliner and pale lipstick. She danced stiffly, a pretty smile pasted onto her pretty face. She never turned around, but now and then she dipped and twisted her torso so that we could all have a look at the rose tattooed on her shoulder blade. She was dancing with a big boy, blond, with a Marine haircut. His muscle shirt was tucked into a pair of Dockers tucked into a pair of combat boots, and he didn't dance so much as stand in place rippling muscled parts of his body. A bulldog quivered on his left shoulder, and a black panther stalked across his chest. When he bumped into a skate punk with a multicolored mohawk, the dance floor turned into a combination brawl and mosh pit, and the bouncer waded into the thick of things to sort it all out. His name was Martinez, according to the Old English lettering arcing across the back of his neck, and he emerged from the melee with a skate punk tucked under each arm. Both biceps were tattooed with barbed-wire bands.

"Are you having a good time?" John asked.

"Not so much," I said. "I guess I should feel right at home, but I truly hate it here."

"You know what the problem is?" John asked.

I waited for an answer. He dragged it out, lighting a cigarette and tracing circles with his index finger in the condensation from his beer bottle.

"We're not like them." He waved the bottle toward the dance floor. "Bunch of fuckin' wannabes. How much shit did you take for being tattooed before it was a cool thing to do? Huh? A whole lot, I bet. And now what? Teenyboppers worshipping you for all the wrong reasons. The worst part is that you—we—don't fit anywhere. Can't hobnob with the plastic yuppie crowd, can't hang with this bunch of tattooed losers, either."

The music sped up, angry notes from a Seattle band. A woman in a leopard-print bolero jacket leapt onto the dance floor. She had matching daggers tattooed on both forearms, and her pierced nostril was connected to her earring by a length of gold chain. She danced a loose peek-a-boo hip-hop shuffle, peering around the daggers on her raised arms with a determinedly dangerous look on her chained face.

There wasn't even a live band. Just speakers on top of speakers and no deejay in sight, no one personally responsible for the throbbing, synthesized drumbeat that penetrated the smoke and the angst like an ice pick through the eardrum. I scrunched my eyes against the clouds of musk-scented smoke that belched out-of-time from the mirrored ball above the dance floor. I felt trapped in some sort of Generation X purgatory, sentenced to an eternity of gratuitous tattoos and bad music.

When the beer gave way to tequila, John licked my neck and sprinkled it with salt. "Open your mouth."

I did, and he stuck a lime wedge, rind in, between my teeth.

"There are spies and subversives everywhere." He lifted his glass for the toast, licked the salt off my neck, tossed back a shot of tequila, and sucked the lime out of my mouth.

That was the second time he kissed me.

"I can't figure you out," John said, "and it pisses me off. When you first came into my shop, I thought you were Mary Poppins, you were so fucking nice."

"Mary Poppins?"

He tipped his head and gave me a half smile. "A dark Mary Poppins, but yeah. Like you half expect everybody to fall in love with you and cry whenever they don't, and like you half don't give a shit what people think. You've got that sweet smile and perky disposition, but there's this darkness oozing out from underneath the Mary Poppins bullshit. That's what I can't figure out."

"I don't know what to tell you," I said. "I'm not dark, but I'm not Mary Poppins, either. People don't make a habit of falling in love with me, and I hardly ever cry."

He was ready to leave when I was, and we smiled with feigned surprise at the pretended coincidence. In the parking lot, he lifted me onto the hood of somebody's 1972 Roadrunner and kissed me. I kissed him back and considered the repercussions, weighing the necessity of my job at the Acme Tattoo against the immediacy of desire.

"Give me a ride home?" he asked. "No big deal, just a ride. Nothing else."

"A ride home. That's it."

When he kissed me the third time, I was standing in the doorway of his bedroom and didn't care what it meant. He held me out at arm's length, pulled me close, and kissed me again.

"I'm a part of you," he said.

"It's the part I don't like very much," I admitted.

"Yes you do."

"No."

"Liar." He smiled. "You like it a lot."

"No."

His tongue swirled along my collarbone, and he bit at the skin covering my jugular vein. "You like this."

"Maybe."

"And this." He slid his hand along my ribs and my breasts, kissed me slow and tender, grabbed the neck of my shirt, and tore it wide open. It was a twenty-five-dollar

T-shirt my ex-husband had purchased at the Gap. *You like this.* Not a question, just words floating toward my ear as he crouched in front of me and unzipped my pants.

"You're just like me," he said, and bit my neck. Hard.

 $\mathcal{P}$AUL SAID, "hello" and I said, "what?" Paul said hello again, said his name with the measured cadence most people reserve for stroke victims or autistics, and tacked a couple words onto that. "Your ex-husband." I expected divorce papers to work like an eraser, eradicating the trail of mistakes that had culminated in broken vows and legal paperwork as well as the (painfully obvious, in retrospect) misguided sentiments that caused us to think we'd been in love with each other in the first place.

One phone call turned into two, and two turned into something like friendship. At first it was veiled jabs and defensive satire and a lot of pretending we hadn't broken each other's hearts. There was something compulsory about the phone calls, and our conversations became more amicable, as though we were required to fill awkward long-distance silences with forced niceties because we'd been the only two soldiers in the matrimonial brigade who'd survived that last enemy raid.

Paul was dating with a vengeance, as though enough women would undo whatever the divorce papers hadn't, as though enough sex would obliterate the stain of our failed marriage. I didn't blame him, even laughed out loud at his stories of the hijinks and conquests that marked his return to bachelor freedom. The details of what I'd been doing and with whom were delivered with the same sense of be-mused detachment, something like *Oh, hi, I'm doing fine, still tattooing, falling in love with my boss. How 'bout yourself?*

Paul called back the next day. "Do you know what he's done?"

"Who?" I asked.

"Your boss. The person you say you're falling in luh-uve with."

"You don't have to be hateful about it," I said. "I'm happy for you and what's-her-name."

"Grand larceny," Paul said. "Burglary. Kidnapping. And those are just the highlights."

"And?"

"I looked up some of the cases," Paul said. "Not all of them, of course. Who'd have the time? Let's just go for the big one, leave the property crimes out of it. He served eight years for kidnapping his girlfriend."

"He did his time, though," I said. "Right? I'm sure it's not something he'd repeat, and she's not his girlfriend any-more. Sounds like a different version of the divorce game."

"Your boss," Paul said, "is a convicted felon."

"You don't know him," I said, "and you don't know me. Not like you ever did." In the demilitarized zone be-tween divorce and friendship, many phone calls ended with words that might have to be eaten later and abrupt dial tones instead of good-byes.

Later that night, John showed up with a dozen roses, a tomahawk he hung above my door, and half a fifth of tequila.

"Would you do something for me?" I asked.

"Anything."

"I took out my nipple rings when I got married. I want them back."

"I don't want to hurt you." He shook his head.

"I don't want you to hurt me, either, but I want my nipples repierced, and I want you to do it."

We drove up the mountain to John's cabin. He organized his piercing gear on the kitchen table, two fourteen-gauge needles, two corks, a smear of Bacitracin on a paper plate, a sterile clamp, gloves, a bottle of Betadine, and a handful of cotton balls. I wandered past him, the memory of having my nipples pierced the first time playing out like a frame-by-frame flashback of a horrific hallucination. I picked up things and put them down, antsy and nervous. Finally I stood in front of the living-room window, arms crossed and foot tapping, staring at the exquisite pine-forest view, trying to think about anything besides piercing.

John's arms slid around me like snakes, squeezing as he kissed my neck. Hands running over me like water, the warmth of his body behind me from head to toe, the fresh tattoo on his arm warmer than the rest of him everywhere it touched.

Two straight-back wooden chairs were facing one another in the kitchen. I sat down and John pulled his chair close, trapping my knees. He unbuttoned my shirt and kissed each nipple before tipping brown Bacitracin onto cotton balls. I reached down and felt for the rungs of the chair, tightening my hands into fists around the carved dowel. I shrank back when the cold clamp touched my flesh, but there wasn't much room for shrinking. John locked the clamp, and the pressure was excruciating.

I shut my eyes.

"Deep breaths, baby. Come on. Breathe for me." John had one gloved hand on the clamps and the other pressed reassuringly on my chest between my breasts. I breathed as best I could. I didn't open my eyes.

"On three." The reassuring warmth of his hand was gone and there was only the clamp and the knowledge that John's other hand was poised near my breast with a sharp, painful object. *I must be out of my mind,* I thought. *Seriously deranged.* I couldn't think why I would have gotten my nipples pierced once, couldn't imagine why doing it again had seemed like a good idea. "One, two, three," a staccato count on one breath and a sudden flash of agony, like fire. As John released the clamp, I looked down at the needle in my nipple and looked away fast. I couldn't get enough air. John leaned forward to cradle my face in his hands.

"You're gray," he said. "Are you okay? You going to pass out?" I shook my head. We waited like that a minute, his hands on my face and his eyes inches from mine, frozen. Then John hooked the jewelry into the end of the needle, slid everything through, and fastened the captive ball. Blood dripped down the side of the hoop.

"Let's wait on the second one." John began to button my shirt.

"What do you mean?"

"That was pretty rough. Why don't we wait a while before we do the second one, maybe let this one heal up first."

"No way," I said. I pulled my shirt open and stared at him. "Do it now." I sounded like a totally tough chick, but what I meant was that it was more a now-or-never thing for me.

"You've got one hell of a set of balls." John shook his head admiringly and picked up the clamps.

I shut my eyes.

"On three." One, two — *blam.*

"Ow," I yelled.

John laughed and I fell forward onto the floor, landing on my knees with my face against John's belly, as the kitchen swirled around me.

"You said three," I mumbled. "I would have been ready on three."

We finished off the tequila and waltzed naked through the cabin. It was bright as daylight outside, a full moon and three feet of new snow.

"Come on," he said, tugging on his boots. "It's beautiful out there."

I started to get dressed.

"No, come like that. Just get some boots."

We stood on the porch, naked from the ankles up. The snow had stopped falling, the wind had stopped blowing, and everything seemed suspended in time.

John picked his way down the steps and across the snow-covered yard until he reached the biggest snowdrift.

He turned around, held both arms straight out, and fell backwards into the snow. He flapped his arms and legs wildly. "I love you," he said, over and over. When he stood up, he left a perfect snow angel behind him.

I KNEW I COULD count on Slade to be more objective than Paul. He'd known me longer, knew me better. He was also newly single, and that world of hurt had been compounded by physical pain and worse. He'd taken up skydiving in California. His goal was to have two hundred jumps before his thirty-fifth birthday. He almost made it. In 1996, a handful of jumps short, a month before his birthday, he jumped out of a plane, expecting his parachute to function as it always had. The main parachute didn't open.

I imagine him calmly looking at the ground, calmly reaching for the cord that would release the reserve chute. I can't picture what happened after that.

The reserve parachute tangled in the useless fabric of the main parachute, and Slade hit the ground hard, breaking his back. The doctors said that he'd never walk again, but they didn't know him very well.

His wreck and his paralysis had all been too much for Lauren, though, and she bailed out on Slade. She wasn't about to marry someone broken. Slade sold the Tattoo Zoo and got a job working in Roseville, at a shop called Wild Bill's, and he'd gone from wheelchair to crutches to cane. Sometimes he acted like the cane belonged to someone else, just because he could. He called it land-surfing, flinging his really bad leg around his sort-of-bad leg, arms outstretched for balance, and it was hard to believe that he used to look like the Marlboro Man. He had girl underpants and a rubber substitute for his ass because the ongoing atrophy of his muscle system had wasted his old butt down to the bone.

Being with John, I explained to Slade, was like visiting someplace I used to live. The smell of his skin reminded me of something I had lost that might be mine again.

Slade started to sing the theme song from *Mystery Date*, opera style. I ignored him. When John touched me, I confided, I was filled with wistful memories and lust, nearly choking from the strength of the sensation.

"Sounds like your soul mate," Slade said, after I'd poured out my heart. I leaned back on the couch, vindicated, a self-satisfied smile warming my face as I pressed the phone hard against my ear. "Soul mate, stalker, psychopath," Slade said. "It's a fine, fine line, isn't it, doll?"

I wished then that I hadn't told Slade about John's time in prison, what he'd done time for.

"I just don't want to see the two of you on the evening news in six months," Slade said, "especially not if one of you is in a body bag and the other's just a mug shot and an all-points bulletin. Know what I'm saying?"

I didn't answer.

"Look," Slade said, "if you love him, I love him for you, but he sounds like the kind of bad idea most people don't walk away from."

"Maybe," I said. "But maybe some people don't want to."

FALLING IN LOVE couldn't change the fact that John was scheduled to stand trial in District Court, that his attorney planned to refute the prosecution's felon-in-possession-of-firearms charge with the argument that the handguns John had pawned months earlier weren't, technically, his. It didn't look good. The week before the hearing was an uneasy combination of sex and Jack Daniels, punctuated by unswerving declarations of love.

"If I get popped," John said, "I'm going to ask the judge for a few days to get my affairs in order. Seeing as how I'm a business owner and all—not a flight risk—I think he'll go for it." This was six hours before his trial, neither of us able to sleep, just lying in bed with our eyes closed in the dark.

"And then," he said, "I'm going to jet right on out of here. Good-bye. And it's *on*. I'd rather live the rest of my life looking over my shoulder than go back to the pen." He wrapped his arm around my waist. "I'm sorry, if that's what it comes down to. I love you, but I'm not going back to prison."

"Maybe I could go with you," I said.

"Really?" His arm jerked upward and settled around my neck. "You'd do that?"

I thought about it, seriously, for a minute. "Sure," I said. "I'd do it."

"For real?" He searched my eyes. "The prison shrink

said they've got a word for people like me." "'*Predator*,'" John said. "'Fuckin' A,' I told him. 'I like being at the top of the food chain.'"

"I don't even eat meat," I said.

"You know what would happen to you, right? Aiding and abetting's probably the least of it."

I nodded and rolled my face into the crook of his elbow, eyelashes touching a tattoo I'd given him. "Probably," I said.

"You'd do it anyway, wouldn't you."

It wasn't a question, but I said yes again.

John kissed the top of my head. "We'll ride off into the sunset and become the king and queen of tattooing," he said.

BEING ON THE RUN from the law was not as exciting as one might imagine. John's definition of "on the run" involved parking a panel truck in my backyard and moving his two big dogs and a duffel bag of clothing into my house. Three blocks from the police station.

WE WERE CAMPING in the mountains west of town when I told John I was pregnant. He couldn't have been more pleased with himself.

"We'll get married, of course," he said. "I'm gonna turn myself in, do my time, so the kid never has to see me in the prison visitation room. And I want to meet your folks. I've got to tell your dad I'll always do right by you."

I wanted to believe him, but he didn't seem in any big

hurry to do this. Instead, he packed up and moved south,
one town—one hide-out—at a time, and before I got a
chance to find out if he was a man of any part of his word,
the police caught up with him in southern Colorado.

The cops, John said, had hauled him out of a beautician's chair, cape and all, mid-haircut. John, the cops said,
had been hauled out of a beautician's waterbed, naked,
mid-coitus. I figured the truth was somewhere in between
since the telling of lies was the one thing John and cops had
in common. He was in Laramie, that's what mattered, and
his mother had bonded him out, which meant we didn't
have to skulk and hide, didn't have to lay low.

The last time I saw John was the day after he got out of
jail. The "outlaw" tattoo on his belly was hidden beneath
a black T-shirt emblazoned with a knockoff of the
Harley Davidson logo, only where it
should have said "Harley Davidson
Motorcycles," it said "Highly Dangerous Motherfucker" instead. The
afternoon played out like a Lifetime: Television for Women western, and by the time it was close to over,
I was wiping blood out of my eyes and
John was waving a gun. Actually, *bran-
dishing* was more like it, brandishing the gun like a western-
movie bad guys.

"So there was this woman," John said, "who found a
rattlesnake. It was hurt, injured somehow, and she took it
home and nursed it back to health. She fed it and cared for

it—loved it, even—and they lived together in harmony for a long, long time." John paused to check my reaction, light a cigarette, and brandish the gun a little bit more.

"Anyway, one day, she reaches down to pet the snake, and the snake sinks its fangs into her wrist. She falls down, of course, clutching her bloody hand while the venom courses through her body, and the snake slithers around until it's even with her head. The two of them are eye to eye, and with her last, dying breath, the woman says, 'How could you do that to me after all I've done for you?' The snake shrugs its little snaky shoulders and says, 'Hey, you knew I was a snake when you picked me up.'"

John pointed the gun at me and then pointed it at the door. "You know the way out."

It sounded like a dare, so I didn't move.

"Go," he said. "Go on. Leave if you're leaving."

I walked very slowly. When my fingers touched the knob, I heard the trigger cock behind me, and I could feel a burst of giggles swelling in my stomach. I wasn't sure what sparked it—John's melodrama, or the idea that this was the kind of scared that could make a person lose touch with reality and never find the way back—but if I laughed, he'd shoot me for sure. That thought turned the giggles into pity so intense it was all I could do not to turn around and hug him good-bye. A foot taller, a hundred pounds heavier, and this was the best he could do, whupping on a pregnant woman.

"Hey." He drew the word out for three or four syllables, infusing it with a growling threat.

I closed my eyes, pity turning to fear awash in waves of pain and sadness. *Please, God,* I thought, *don't let him be the kind of person who would shoot an unarmed pregnant woman in the back of the head. Don't let him be that much of a coward.*

"If you go to the cops," he said, "if you tell anyone, I'll fuckin' bury you."

I nodded. I heard the trigger ease down into a safer place. I opened the door and walked to my car. I drove slowly, half expecting a bullet to shatter the rear window and explode the back of my head.

I went to my obstetrician's office to make sure the baby was okay. The baby was fine, and I lied big when the doctor asked what had happened. Then I went home, took out the only picture I had of John, and looked at it hard. It was like looking at a stranger. I hadn't known it would be possible to fall out of love in an instant, but that's what had happened. I wondered whether a real outlaw would wear a "Highly Dangerous Motherfucker" T-shirt. I wondered whether a real outlaw, if I ever met one, would have a tattoo label.

I thought about leaving town, leaving the state, but Laramie was my home. If I was going to be on the run from a fake outlaw who was on the run from the law, I might as well do it here.

Epilogue

The last tattoo I did at Zowie was on a Saturday night. Savic and Karen were loading up and heading out and there was only so much time left. A cluster of college girls in one corner were giggling and pointing out which flash designs they'd *never* get.

"Can I help you find something?" I asked.

"You work here?" one of them asked.

"Yeah. There are more designs in the binders on the coffee table," I said, "or we can draw anything you want."

"But you're pregnant," she said. Her two friends giggled uncomfortably.

"Really?" I looked down. "Wonder how that happened."

"Well, um, do you have any pictures of, like, those Japanese symbols?"

"The ones that mean stuff," one of the others added.

"Congi? Sure." I led them to the congi flash on the opposite wall. A few minutes later, all three made up their minds. All three wanted the symbol for "nonconformist" on precisely the same place on their ankles.

I remember the back and forth of it all, the little circles of shading. Working with the grain of the skin and holding the stretch tight, tight, tight. Savic was packing up furniture with a vengeance and muttering to himself. He eyed the stool I was sitting on with vivid impatience, and I could tell he was imagining it beneath a different employee in a different shop in a different town as far from Laramie as the U-Haul truck could carry him.

I began to tattoo the outline on the first nonconformist symbol, and it wasn't long before the questions
started, the usual ones. *How long have you been doing this?* I
answered honestly, but thought the first nonconformist
should have asked this one before she let me start poking her with needles. *How'd you get started?* I amused the
second nonconformist with anecdotes of apprenticeship, stories of tattooing grapefruit and bananas and
Styrofoam cups. *Why?*

"There's a story for you," I said. As I wiped down
the third nonconformist's tattoo, I calculated the minutes before it would be finished. I remember thinking,
There's just enough time.

In 1978, the summer I was fifteen, my father
elected to drive through Canada for our last-ever family
vacation in a Volare station wagon with imitation
wood-grain side panels. After a week of sightseeing in
what passed for a foreign country, we stopped for ice
cream and gas in a town called Kamloops. I was standing in the shade of the gas station watching sap drip
from a big stand of trees, clacking the side of my Dr.
Scholl sandal against the curb and sucking a twist-top
out of its cone while waves of gasoline fumes and heat
rose through the air.

I heard the motorcycles before I saw them. A low rumble vibrated the asphalt under my feet like a freight train. A dozen motorcycles poured into the parking lot, and men and women with windblown hair tumbled off in a whirlwind of black leather and dust. The leader of the pack leaned back on his long, low chopper. His beard had been parted by the wind, and his fur-covered helmet looked like a bouffant gone bad. He was a wild, magical man. A creature. His lanky legs were poured into tight black jeans, and the shoulder seams of his jacket were frayed where the sleeves had once been at-tached. And there, on his arm, was the apparent source of his magic. A tattooed snake curled around his biceps and disappeared into his armpit. The tattooed snake undulated as he pulled a bandanna from his pocket and wiped the sweat from his neck. I stared past the hor-rified look on my mother's face and caught his eye through the heat waves rising from the asphalt. He looked right at me. Into me, it seemed. The snake rippled and flexed as he patted his thigh and cocked his head, daring and inviting.

My mother told me to get into the car *this instant.* I looked at the car and I looked at the man on the mo-torcycle. For a moment, I fantasized about running

across the parking lot in slow motion, climbing on behind him and riding away, never looking back. I imagined a carefree life with him and his tattooed snake,
doing whatever it is that outlaws do. I didn't take my
eyes off him as I opened the car door and climbed in.
His lips curled into a smile that was half sinister and
half angelic, mocking and forgiving. The sun glinted off
his gold-capped tooth.

I sat in the backseat with my face glued to the window, mesmerized, as the station wagon pulled out
of the parking lot. The motorcycles got smaller and
smaller, disappearing altogether when we rounded a
curve near the highway. The heat, the ice cream, the
sandals—everything faded away as I savored the dangerous, splendid taste of that moment. I closed my eyes
and pictured that man's face. In my mind, he came
closer and closer to me, leaning over me and smiling
with open lips.

Somehow I'd managed to get through fifteen years
without ever seeing a tattoo, without even thinking
about tattoos or the people who had them. The snake
tattoo melded into the rest of the outlaw image, until all
the elements of what I'd seen took on heroic propor-
tions. *It all made sense; of course outlaw heroes ride motorcycles*

now, I thought. *All that asphalt—even a town girl knows that
blacktop is hard on hooves.*

"I spent the trip home staring sullenly out the window, thinking about tattoos and outlaws and wishing I
had one of each," I said. The nonconformists' tattoos
were done and bandaged, and I ended the story with a
sad little Mona Lisa smile, just like always, as though
there had been no turning back for a girl like me after
something like that, as though that moment had been a
jumping-off point.

As though I'd been pushed.

The third nonconformist nodded with the faraway
smile of a person who's wondering what moment of
her own past will turn out to be so sharply defining.
Savic whisked the tattoo stool out from under me and
loaded it into the truck.

I've told the same story so many times that I can't
be sure when fact gave way to exaggeration, interpola-
tion, and bold-faced lies. One thing I know for sure is
that the only cause-and-effect salience of this anecdote
was tacked on in retrospect somewhere along the way,
a seamless and meaningful addition. I've told this story
so many times that I can picture it like yesterday, the
story version more vivid than the forgotten memories

of whatever actually happened, negating what, if anything, it really meant.

It's not a purposeful lie. I've only told the story to people who paid me for a tattoo, so it's customer service, really. They've paid for the mark and the experience of getting tattooed and the memories that go along with it. They've invested in future nostalgia. They've paid for years' worth of storytelling, tales about why they got a particular tattoo and what the tattoo meant and whether it still does; how it felt and how it faded; whether it was, in retrospect, regrettably foolish or the best thing they've ever done, and why. Given enough time, they'll get around to me, and that's when my story gets wrapped up in theirs. Chances are, their stories improve with this addition; the woman who tattooed them, in the nostalgic transformations of actual events, can be described as having run away with a renegade band of outlaw bikers at a tender age. This, of course, has everything to do with how they wound up getting a tattoo from me.

On the way home, I stopped at the grocery store where I've shopped for most of my adult life. I was standing in front of the bakery counter, peering through the tiny blue squares of an empty shopping basket balanced on top of my belly, eying an assortment of baked goods.

"Can I help you?" A woman in a white baker's uniform brushed the flour from her hands and waited on her side of the counter. When I didn't answer right away, she followed the trajectory of my stare. "That's tiramisù," she said. "Liqueur-flavored cake with mocha whipped cream between the layers."

"It's supposed to be ladyfingers and espresso and mascarpone cheese," I said, "and the liqueur is supposed to be real. Why is it here?"

"It's very popular," she answered defensively. "You really should try some."

"Okay." I didn't want to argue, and I felt bad for hurting her feelings.

I wandered through the store, my basket empty except for the tiramisù. I'd had the traditional version a time or two in San Francisco; that's how I knew about the ladyfingers. I liked it just fine, and I supposed I'd eat this piece sooner or later. I was just a little disconcerted. I'd never thought that Laramie would turn into the kind of town that needed tiramisù, imitation or otherwise.

I stopped in front of a display of clearance items, toys mostly, and found the only thing that could have surprised me more than the local availability of fancy city desserts: Butterfly Art Barbie. She was wearing a tiny, Barbie-pink-and-yellow crocheted bikini top and a denim skirt that barely covered her Barbie ass over the matching, crocheted bikini bottom. Between the bikini top and the skirt, this Barbie had a Barbie-pink-and-yellow butterfly tattoo that spanned the narrow width of her tummy. The box didn't say "Tattoo Art Barbie," but that's what she was, no mistake about it. She even came with "decorations" for her owner, temporary tattoos of butterflies and flowers.

I put Butterfly Art Barbie in the basket with the tiramisù and headed for the checkout line, wondering what the people at Mattel could have been thinking. They might as well have labeled her Trailer Trash Barbie, the way they dressed her. If it had been up to me, I'd have let the tattoo be a surprise beneath the clothing of Business Suit Barbie. That's how it works most of the time in real life.

I took my tiramisù and my Butterfly Art Barbie home and put them both in the refrigerator so I wouldn't have to look at either one of them again, at least not right away, but every time I opened the refrigerator door to pour a glass of milk or get a piece of beef jerky, the little light came on, and there they were. Every time I opened the refrigerator door, I was caught in the high beams of my own derisive insights.

$\mathcal{I}$T'S BEEN ALMOST four years since Zowie Tattoo was loaded into a Georgia-bound U-Haul, and I'm now the mother of a three-and-a-half-year-old son. The last days of Zowie, like most everything else that came before Sam, fade in comparison. I've spent years looking at the world through Sam's eyes, wrapped up in an irony-free perspective of things. Sam is big on taking time to notice whatever most people don't have time to bother with, like the changing sounds of a train whistle on the wind or the colors of clouds.

Like most three-year-olds, Sam is the embodiment of the mythical western outlaw. His world is one of absolutes and injustices in which compromise is rarely an option. Lately, Sam has been in the process of scrutinizing issues of ownership, and like any self-respecting outlaw, his code of ethics leaves little room for legal rights or logic. Sam's side of things boils down to "I had it first," a philosophy liberally applied to everything from toys to Nilla wafers, from the choking hazards of a carburetor-rebuild kit to the running-with-scissors possibilities of pinking shears.

I had it first. Even if his hand wasn't on it, even if he'd never seen anything like it and wasn't sure what it was or did, even if it was nothing more than déjà vu or possibility, Sam had it first. There's no room in any "I had it first" argument for rational thinking or facts; it's like nostalgia that way.

"I had it first," Sam says, and there's an edge to his voice as though he's daring me to say otherwise. "I'm talking to my daddy." Sam holds his hand over the mouthpiece to whisper this to me, pulls the phone into the kitchen for privacy. The phone isn't plugged into anything, and Sam thinks his daddy is a guy named Kowalski, the main character in *Vanishing Point,* the only grown-up movie he's ever seen.

Vanishing Point isn't much more than ninety-nine minutes of chase scenes and the sound of a 1970 Challenger engine. A simple misunderstanding snowballs into an all-points bulletin and every cop from Denver to Truckee gunning for Kowalski, who becomes a folk hero in the process because the injustice of it all is narrated by a blind disc jockey broadcasting on radio station KOW. On the screen, Kowalski's narrow escapes are punctuated with flashback scenes that are supposed to add up to the way he turned into this particular kind of outlaw. He's eventually cornered, caught between a battalion of cop cars and a bulldozer roadblock. Kowalski turns the Challenger toward the bulldozers, peels out with the throttle wide open, and never looks back. Sheet-metal shrapnel falls like slow-motion rain against a backdrop of small explosions framed by the impassive faces of small-town folk. (Sam and I don't watch that part. *Vanishing Point,* at our house, is more like ninety inconclusive minutes of muscle-car mayhem.)

The first time Sam saw *Vanishing Point,* he was supposed to be napping. I didn't know he'd crept into the living room until the first close-up of Kowalski flickered on the television. Sam sucked in his breath, pointed, and said, "Daddy."

I started in with my usual explanation about daddies and how some kids have dads and some kids don't, but Sam wasn't having any of that. "That is my daddy," he said, over and over until we were reduced to an is-not/is-too exchange. I lost.

Every few months, Sam asks if we can watch his daddy movie, and we do. In between, Sam talks to

Kowalski (or maybe it's somebody else) on a broken telephone and reports back. *Daddy loves us. Daddy's car is real fast. Daddy wants a doggie, just like Sam. Daddy's coming to our house,* Sam confides, *but not today.* It's always *not today,* but Sam never seems to mind.

In real life, the absent father skipped out on another sentencing hearing and another bail bond before Sam was born. The police haven't caught up with him, not that they've much bothered trying. The absent father is no Kowalski. I used to wonder how many years the absent father would have to spend looking over his shoulder before he realized there'd never be anyone there, wondered if he'd feel lonely or foolish when it happened, but now he's faded into the same kind of nothing as someone else's bad dream.

ABOUT THE TIME Sam began to apply his outlaw philosophy to issues of ownership, nostalgia snuck up on me and settled in for a few weeks. It was more like an infomercial than a stroll down memory lane; it was a montage of fast-cut edits and images spliced together MTV-style with a spaghetti-western soundtrack. I was left with a blissful version of my past that must have originated somewhere between Never-Never Land and heaven, a nostalgic reminiscence of a time or a place in which there was an outlaw for every girl, all tattoos were works of art, and happy endings waited around each corner.

Nostalgia is a compelling emotion, more so than love, even, or hate, and it's almost always bittersweet, like death or an orgasm. Nostalgia is sneaky. It tries to pass itself off as a journalist reporting back from your past, likes to dress up like the nonfiction section of your public library. Nostalgia likes to watch you root through boxes and dresser drawers, searching for souvenirs and evidence. The ticket stubs, the pressed wedding bouquet, the bundles of old letters in which only you can read the love between the lines. If it sticks around long enough, it rearranges the meanings of the artifacts of your memories and draws conclusions about your past with the certainty of a three-year-old child.

Nostalgia is where memories and desire overlap, and it's easy to get lost in a place like that

$\mathcal{I}$ WAS BORN in Tanzania—in Africa—and for most of my life, this was the most exotic thing about me. When I was the new kid in second grade at Nellie Iles Elementary in Laramie, Wyoming, I milked my birthplace

for all it was worth. I acted as though I had just stepped off the plane, wearing my mother's dashikis as often as possible and carrying my parents' souvenirs to every show-and-tell. I implied that these things were used in our household on a daily basis, as though my typical afternoon snack was a blend of warm milk and fresh cow's blood sipped from a bota bag made from the stomach of a goat.

I wanted to be special, a sparkling stone in a box of dull rocks.

Maybe I grew up western without really noticing, Calamity Jane without a horse, or maybe that's just something else I've said so often enough that it sounds like the truth. When I was very young, I believed that the West was special, that Wyoming was the Indian word for a land where courageous men and strong women struggled against the hardships of isolation and nature, carving out a peculiarly western code of ethics and morality along the way.

But this was accompanied by the unspoken belief

that the West was the kind of special place in which someone like me didn't belong.

For the first twenty years of my life, I never felt especially western. I didn't have any of the accoutrements associated with the myth—no horse, no boots, no hat. I was a town girl. My mother's cousin was from a third-generation ranching family whose homesteaded land was forty-five miles or so from Laramie, but it wasn't like I begged to go visiting. That ranch, like any other, was another reminder of just how western I wasn't.

I hated the West when I was younger, loathed Laramie with the intensity of an animal that would have chewed off one leg or another to free itself from a steel-jawed trap. I hated the cloying smallness of town, and I feared the gaping expanse of prairie as well as the mountain ranges that loomed like molars above the sagebrush. And then there was the wind, the Wyoming wind that shoved more than a few homesteaders over the brink of insanity. The wind hurls icy taunts in February, breaks and enters in March, spits a phlegm of sleet in April. The rest of the year, it just blows.

———

I STARTED OUT with the same untattooed skin as everybody else, the same two thousand years of history of place and mark, and stayed in the West, tattooed and tattooing, until both place and mark felt like mine.

When I started getting tattooed, cowboys hurled insults from pickup trucks at me, yelling "freak" or worse, and college boys mistook my tattoos for a semiotic invitation to rearrange the boundaries of my clothing. I've been getting tattooed since before tattooing was popular, long enough to have a nostalgic, childlike sense of ownership. It's the same way I feel about Wyoming. The West gets under your skin eventually, stays as long as a tattoo. It's a parasite-host relationship, but it's hard to tell which is which. I stay because I know the outer limits of the hardness of this place, and because it's more beautiful in its severity than easier places I've seen. I claim it with the petulant certainty of a small child. I didn't want it until someone else picked it up, and then I wailed because I had it first.

Tattooed and western, that's how I've described myself for most of my adult life. I felt more tattooed with each fifty-dollar, first-time tattoo I did, more western with each person who moved to Laramie from someplace else. I defined myself with a superficial and self-serving piety based on nothing more than the context of relativity and the reflection of other people's admiration for the two things about me that are most obvious and least complex. In reality, I'm sort of tattooed and kind of western, and I spent years playing it up into something big.

When did I stop thinking of myself as an artist? I wonder. Tattooed and western, the sum total of my experiences, the distillation of my being, half-truths, my epitaph. If it were completely untrue, a calculated deception, there'd be a pathological pride to it all. If it were completely true, I don't know what it would mean.

I am a microcosm of everything I despise.

ᏞUCKILY, THERE is Sam. The other day, when Sam and I walked outside, he stopped and sucked in his breath and pointed. "The moon," he said. "Look, Mom, my moon." It was the middle of the afternoon, but there it was, the moon. "Oh, no," Sam said. "My moon is broken." It looked like a bad tattoo, the outline not quite a full circle, the center lit with lopsided earthshine and pocked with holidays of blue sky.

"I'm going to put on my bird costume," Sam said, "and fly up in the sky to fix the holes in the moon. But

don't worry, Mommy, I'll be right back, and I'm bringing my moon for you. You can keep it in your heart and
you'll be happy always."

This is the most beautiful thing anyone has ever
said to me, it's romantic and idealistic, the kind of
thinking associated with a wild imagination running
amuck, which is the same kind of thinking I've always
attributed to the combination of western myth and
western place. It's an optimism that stems from the
connection between people and an unforgiving landscape, half hope and half faith about what people can
survive and what they might become if they try hard
enough. Maybe this optimism isn't specifically western.
Maybe it's a part of human nature that's too easily forgotten or dismissed, andmaybe holding onto it just
comes easier in Wyoming.

Maybe it's not too late to get it back.

ACKNOWLEDGMENTS

To Warren Frazier, for his quirky imagination and contagious enthusiasm, and to my dad, Ken Griffin, who gave me a place to write and the luxury of both time and furniture — thank you, thank you.

Many thanks to Ann Patty for the gentle precision with which she edited my manuscript, and to David Hough, who knows which pictures are worth a thousand words and which pictures aren't.

I am grateful for the friendship, encouragement, and support of the following people: Anne Hokenstad, Christy Stillwell, RoseMarie London, Cam Holtz, Terri Kindler, Bill Downs, Eric Sandeen, Jason Young, Leah and Sharl Griffin, Beth Wilkinson, Steve and Sandy Adams, and Paul Sonenberg. I also want to thank Julene Bair and the members of the Silver Sage Writers Alliance who critiqued this work in its early stages, and Mike Shay and the Wyoming Arts Council for noticing me when it mattered most.

And, of course, none of this could have happened — on the pages of a book or otherwise — without Slade Fiero. Thanks, buddy.

ILLUSTRATION CREDITS

Page v, art by Karol Griffin
Page viii, postcard courtesy of
 Paul S. Sonenberg
Page 1, art by Karol Griffin
Page 8, postcard courtesy of Back
 of the Wagon Antiques
Page 17, art by Eleanor Dart,
Page 27, art by Karol Griffin
Page 33, art by Karol Griffin
Page 37, art by Karol Griffin
Page 41, artist unknown
Page 49, photograph by Karol
 Griffin
Page 55, art by Karol Griffin
Page 57, photograph by Karol
 Griffin
Page 59, photograph by Karol
 Griffin
Page 64, photograph by Karol
 Griffin
Page 73, photograph by Stephanie
 Silsby
Page 77, art by Karol Griffin
Page 83, art by Karol Griffin
Page 89, photographs by Karol
 Griffin
Page 94, art by Karol Griffin
Page 104, photographer unknown
Page 107, art by Karol Griffin
Page 115, art by Karol Griffin
Page 125, postcard courtesy of
 Paul S. Sonenberg
Page 130, photograph by Ken
 Griffin

Page 133, art by Karol Griffin
Page 142, postcard courtesy of
 Paul S. Sonenberg
Page 149, artist unknown
Page 152, photograph by Ken
 Griffin
Page 162, postcard courtesy of
 Back of the Wagon Antiques
Page 167, art by Karol Griffin
Page 180, postcard courtesy of
 Back of the Wagon Antiques
Page 186, art by Karol Griffin
Page 199, photograph by Karol
 Griffin
Page 203, art by Harley Haslam
Page 209, photograph by Karol
 Griffin
Page 216, art by Karol Griffin
Page 223, tattoo and photograph
 by Terri Kindler
Page 228, photographer unknown
Page 235, art by Karol Griffin
Page 241, postcard courtesy of
 Paul S. Sonenberg
Page 250, postcard courtesy of
 Karol Griffin
Page 252, art by Harley Haslam
Page 254, art and photograph by
 Terri Kindler
Page 272, art by Eleanor Dart
Page 275, art by Harley Haslam
Page 281, art by Savic Enn
Page 290, photograph by Karol
 Griffin